THE LAB MANUAL

to accompany

Henry

THE

SKILLED

READER

Third Edition

Mary Dubbé
Thomas Nelson Community College

Longman

Boston   Columbus   Indianapolis   New York   San Francisco   Upper Saddle River

Amsterdam   Cape Town   Dubai   London   Madrid   Milan   Munich   Paris   Montreal   Toronto

Delhi   Mexico City   São Paulo   Sydney   Hong Kong   Seoul   Singapore   Taipei   Tokyo

The Lab Manual to accompany Henry, *The Skilled Reader, Third Edition*

5 6 7 8 9 10–EBM–13 12

Longman is an
imprint of

www.pearsonhighered.com

ISBN 10: 0-205-82473-0
ISBN 13: 978-0-205-82473-1

CONTENTS

For Students:

This Lab Manual is a collection of 66 activities designed to provide additional practice and enrichment for the skills in *The Skilled Reader*. Each chapter consists of six lab activities that will provide you with additional practice and assessment of your skills.

You will practice applying the strategies you are learning to numerous textbook paragraphs and longer passages from a wide range of academic disciplines. You will continue to learn new vocabulary in many activities, practice identifying main ideas and supporting details, use outlines and concept maps to make sure you understand the reading selections, and practice your inference skills in the contexts of excerpts taken primarily from current college textbooks.

This lab manual also includes a skills awareness inventory sheet for each of the tutorial tests that you may take before you begin the course as well as achievement tests to discover how much you have learned by the end of the course. Three pairs of tests are available: one is specifically designed for students in Florida who must pass the Florida State Basic Skills Exit Test, a second is for Texas students who need to take the THEA, and a third is intended for more general use. (Your instructor will provide the most appropriate one for you.) Answer sheets are available in the back of the Lab Manual as well as report forms that foster metacognition. These report forms can be used as a portfolio activity to help you assess your learning and growth.

Finally, at the end of the manual is a report form where you can record your grades and keep track of your progress. Mastering these skills will ensure that you are effectively prepared for your academic subjects.

For Instructors:

The Lab Manual is a collection of 66 activities designed to provide additional practice and enrichment for the skills in *The Skilled Reader*. Each chapter consists of six lab activities that can be used to add flexibility and interest to the classroom or for additional practice and for assessment purposes.

These lab activities provide students with a range of opportunities to practice becoming skilled readers. The chapters of *The Skilled Reader* include numerous practices, applications, review tests, and mastery tests. The Lab Manual offers two practice exercises, two review tests, and two mastery tests that mirror the design of the text and emphasize the reading skills and applications students need to succeed in college. Students apply the strategies they are learning to numerous textbook paragraphs and longer passages from a wide range of academic disciplines.

Each activity in the Lab Manual is carefully constructed to ensure that students understand the purpose of the activity and can complete it successfully. The practice exercises begin with a succinct statement of the objective. The Answer Key to the Lab Manual can be found online at www.ablongman.com/henry and by choosing *The Skilled Reader*. A report form is available at the end of the manual for students to keep a record of their scores and to track their progress.

The lab manual also includes a skills awareness inventory sheet for each of the tutorial tests that students may take before they begin the course as well as achievement tests to discover how much they have learned by the end of the course. Three pairs of tests are available for students using *The Skilled Reader*: one is specifically designed for students in Florida who must pass the Florida State Basic Skills Exit Test, a second is for Texas students who need to take the THEA, and a third is intended for more general use. The answer sheets are available in the back of the Lab Manual as well as report forms that foster metacognition. These report forms can be used as a portfolio activity to help assess student learning and growth. The tutorial tests appear in the Instructor's Manual that accompanies *The Skilled Reader*, or you can access the tutorial tests by going to http://www.ablongman.com/henry and selecting *The Skilled Reader*.

ABOUT THE SERIES

The Effective Reader, 3e (available in November, 2010)
The Skilled Reader, 3e (available in November, 2010)
The Master Reader, 3e (available in December, 2010)

The series of skills-based textbooks, written by D. J. Henry of Daytona Beach Community College, features plentiful opportunities for students to practice individual and combined reading skills on high-interest passages from both textbooks and popular sources. Basic reading comprehension and vocabulary skills are addressed, and critical reading skills are introduced in careful step-by-step fashion.

The Henry series focuses students' attention on how their skills apply to reading college textbooks. The books also emphasize the importance of visuals, in addition to text, as valuable sources of information. Students are asked to respond to visuals throughout the series in Visual Vocabulary features. The Lab Manual offers 66 activities designed to provide additional practice and enrichment for all the topics in each book.

ABOUT THE LAB MANUAL AUTHOR

This manual is based upon much of the work of Susan Pongratz, who graduated from The College of William and Mary with a B.A. in English and an M.A. in Education. In addition to teaching developmental reading classes at Thomas Nelson Community College and co-coordinating the Verizon Reading Center there, she supervised student teachers for several years at Christopher Newport University. Since completing the Eastern Virginia Writing Project in 2002, she now serves as a teaching consultant, strongly espousing the philosophy of the reading/writing connection.

Mary Dubbé, who authored the revision of this Lab Manual, also teaches reading classes at Thomas Nelson Community College. She graduated from West Virginia University with an M.S. degree in language arts and an M.A. in reading. She has over 25 years of experience in preparing college students to be skilled readers and successful students. In addition to teaching, Mary is the director of learning communities on her campus, has presented workshops at several state and national conferences, and is a past the president of the Virginia Association of Developmental Education.

Chapter 1: A Reading System for Skilled Readers
LAB 1.1 PRACTICE EXERCISE 1

Name _____ Section _____ Date _____ Score (number correct) _____ x 10 = _____

Objective: To practice the SQ3R method of reading and studying.

Directions: Read the following passage and answer the questions that follow.

Two Causes of Abuse in the Family

Parents who abuse their children were often abused themselves. Too often, abused children become abusive parents. To stop the cycle of abuse, the reasons for abuse must be understood. In some cases, *poverty* may breed abuse. Poverty may arise from lack of education, unemployment, or divorce. Lack of money to cover the cost of food, housing, and clothing can cause deep fear and anger, leading to abuse. In other cases, *family stress* may lead to abuse. Poor relationships between parents and children may lead to violence. Alcohol and drug abuse can also lead to family violence.

_____1. Which of the following would be helpful prior knowledge for your understanding of the paragraph?
   a. background about the problems associated with a lack of education
   b. background about unemployment issues
   c. background about family stress
   d. all of the above

_____2. Upon surveying this paragraph, what does the skilled reader first notice?
   a. the phrase "abused children"
   b. the title and the phrases in italics
   c. the phrase "in some cases"
   d. the reasons for poverty

_____3. What is your purpose for reading this paragraph?
   a. to learn about two causes of abuse in families
   b. to gather information about the statistics of abuse and other family problems
   c. to be persuaded to take action against abuse
   d. to distinguish between abuse and punishment

_____4. Which of the following questions best taps into the main ideas of the paragraph?
   a. How can abuse be stopped?
   b. What kinds of problems do most families have?
   c. What are the two causes of abuse in families?
   d. What is the difference between abuse and punishment?

_____5. Why are *poverty* and *family stress* in italics?
   a. These are terms used by the police in describing domestic situations
   b. These are terms used by scientists who conduct research
   c. These are terms used by politicians who are seeking votes
   d. These terms are the two reasons for abuse in families

1

A Need for Change

Retailers are always searching for new marketing strategies to attract and hold customers. In the past, retailers attracted customers with unique products and more or better services. Today, products and services are looking more and more alike. Many national-brand manufacturers, in their drive for sales, have placed their brands almost everywhere. You can find most brands not only in department stores (JCPenney) but also in mass-merchandise discount stores (Wal-Mart), off-price discount stores (TJ Maxx), and on the Web. Thus, it's more difficult for any one retailer to offer exclusive merchandise.

Service differentiation among retailers has also eroded. Many department stores have trimmed their services, whereas discounters have increased theirs. Customers have become smarter and more price sensitive. They see no reason to pay more for identical brands, especially when service differences are shrinking. For all these reasons, many retailers today are rethinking their marketing strategies.

—Adapted from Kotler and Armstrong, *Principles of Marketing*, 13th ed., p. 378.

_____6. Which of the following would be helpful prior knowledge for your understanding of the paragraph?
a. Information about manufacturing costs
b. Information about marketing strategies
c. Information about new trends and fashions
d. Information about the likes and dislikes of retailers

_____7. What is the topic of this passage?
a. trends in sales
b. discount stores
c. department stores
d. changes in retail marketing

_____8. What is your purpose for reading this paragraph?
a. to gather background information about the changes in retail marketing
b. to be entertained by an amusing "shopping" story
c. to make a decision about where to find the best prices
d. to compare and contrast different stores

_____9. Upon surveying this passage, what does the skilled reader notice about the title?
a. The title is very informative.
b. The title does not fit the passage.
c. The title hints at the central idea of the passage, but more information is needed.
d. The title is humorous and catches attention.

_____10. Based upon the information in the paragraph, what is the best definition for *service differentiation*?
a. differences in branches of the military
b. differences in restaurant venues
c. differences in types of services offered by retailers to consumers
d. differences in the types of stores that offer retail merchandise

2

Chapter 1: A Reading System for Skilled Readers
LAB 1.1 PRACTICE EXERCISE 2

Name _____ Section _____ Date _____ Score (number correct) _____ x 10 = _____

Objective: To apply a system of reading to studying from a textbook.

Directions: Read the following passage and answer the questions that follow.

Mind Your Manners and Theirs

The saying, "When in Rome, do as the Romans do," suggests that international travelers should adopt an other oriented approach to the host country's manners and customs. After interviewing hundreds of international businesspeople, Roger Axtell offers the following tips on etiquette when visiting with people from other countries or traveling to international destinations. Realize, of course, that these observations are not true of all individuals. As in the United States, in many of these countries there are dozens of different cultural groups with their own sets of values and customs.

Austrians
- Are punctual
- Use a firm handshake (both men and women)
- Consider keeping their hands in their lap when dining to be impolite
- Are uncomfortable with first names until a friendship is established

English, Scots, Welsh
- Value punctuality
- Are accustomed to cooler room temperatures than Americans
- Call a Scot a Scotsman (or Scotswoman), not a Scotchman or Scottish

French
- Rarely use first names, even among colleagues
- Frequently shake hands, but their grip is less firm than most
- Usually eat their main meal of the day at midday
- Make decisions after much deliberation

Irish
- Are not overly conscientious about time and punctuality
- Do not typically give business gifts
- May regard refusing a drink or failing to buy a round as bad manners

Egyptians
- Like practicing Muslims, rest on Friday
- Regard friendship and trust as a prerequisite for business
- Usually hold social engagements late in the day

Zambians
- Often shake hands with the left supporting the right
- When dining, may ask for food; it is impolite not to
- Consider it improper to refuse food

Indians
- When greeting a woman, put palms together and bow slightly
- Regard the cow as a sacred animal
- Show great respect to elders

Japanese
- Exchange business cards before bowing or shaking hands
- Consider it impolite to have long or frequent eye-to-eye contact
- Rarely use first names
- Avoid the word *no* to preserve harmony

Thais
- Regard displays of either temper or affection in public as unacceptable
- Have a taboo against using your foot to point or showing your sole
- Don't like pats on the head

Brazilians
- Like long handshakes
- Like to touch arms, elbows, and backs
- When conversing, view interruption as enthusiasm
- Attach a sexual meaning to the OK hand signal

Mexicans
- Are not rigidly punctual
- Take their main meal at about 1 or 4 P.M.
- Refrain from using first names until they are invited to do so
- Consider hands in the pockets to be impolite.

—Beebe, Beebe, and Redmond, *Interpersonal Communication: Relating to Others*,
3rd ed., pp. 126–127.

—Axtell, R.E. (1994). *Do's and Taboos Around the World*, 3rd ed., New York: Wiley

_____ 1. All of the following would be helpful prior knowledge for reading this selection *except*
    a. what is considered good manners varies from country to country.
    b. knowing the manners of other countries can be considered good business practice.
    c. the United States does not push studying a foreign language the way other countries emphasize learning English.
    e. the manners listed are not always to be applied to all people in the labeled country.

_____ 2. The following are all questions to consider as you read the passage *except* which one?
    a. Why are English, Scots, and Welsh more accustomed to cooler temperatures than people in the United States?
    b. What is an appropriate business gift for someone from Ireland?
    c. How do the customs of Brazilians differ from those of Mexicans?
    d. Are the customs of Thais and Japanese consistent with the customs of other Asians?

_____ 3. According to the reading, in which country should you avoid greeting your business associate with an affectionate kiss on the cheek?
    a. Thailand   c. Mexico
    b. Brazil   d. France

_____ 4. When attending a business meeting, it would be important to be on time in all of the following countries *except*
    a. Austria.   c. Mexico.
    b. England.   d. Scotland.

_____ 5. It would be considered inappropriate to use the first names of people from which country?
    a. England   c. Austria
    b. Scotland   d. Wales

_____ 6. You would not expect to participate in social activities in the early morning in which country?
    a. Thailand   c. Austria
    b. England   d. Egypt

_____ 7. Business associates of which country would not appreciate a menu that included steak or hamburger?
    a. Brazil   c. India
    b. Mexico   d. Ireland

_____ 8. In which country might some people want you to ask for food?
    a. Egypt   c. Zambia
    b. India   d. Thailand

_____ 9. You would try to avoid eye-to-eye contact with people from what country?
    a. England   c. Brazil
    b. Japan   d. France

_____ 10. "Failing to buy your round" in Ireland means
    a. failing to buy drinks for everyone in the group.
    b. failing to pay for one golf game.
    c. failing to pay for a game of pool.
    d. failing to bring a gift for the host.

Chapter 1: A Reading System for Skilled Readers
LAB 1.3 REVIEW TEST 1

Name _____ Section _____ Date _____ Score (number correct) _____ x 10 = _____

Directions: Use skilled reading to answer the questions that follow this passage.

Promoting Change

Threats

1 Interested in improving your health? Concerned about the water you drink, the food you eat, or catching a new infectious disease like SARS or bird flu? If so, you are not alone. At no time in our nation's history have so many individuals, government agencies, community groups, policymakers, businesses, and health organizations focused so intently on a growing list of health-related issues. Epidemic rates of **obesity** and **diabetes**, a growing list of infectious and chronic diseases, a wide range of environmental threats, and other health problems are highlighted daily in the popular media. This widespread focus on health problems can make even the most healthy among us wonder what we can do to protect ourselves and our loved ones.

Advertising Issues

2 Juxtaposed against these very real threats to our health are the advertisements that offer pharmaceutical help for almost any problem. Drugs designed to help you get a full night of sleep, increase sexual responsiveness, reduce our levels of cholesterol, and eliminate stress, depression, or anxiety have exploded on the market. Books touting the newest "low-carb" fix for obesity and fitness regimens promising to give you that "six-pack stomach" fly from bookstore shelves. We are told that there are solutions to our health problems, and are led to believe that the fix is only a pill away.

Conflicting Information

3 For many of us our health is a priority, and millions of us are working hard to try to change our lifestyles and improve our health. On a daily basis we are challenged to "Just do it, but don't overdo it"; "Be all you can be, but be yourself"; "Consider soy milk instead of regular dairy"; "Cut the bad carbs and bad fat, increase the good carbs and good fat" and "Eat more fruits and vegetables, but make sure they are organic"—and "If you want to look and feel good, exercise, exercise, exercise!" Clearly, conflicting health claims abound, and we must learn to decipher health fads from truly reputable information. We often assume that the government, pharmaceutical industry, and medical profession will protect us or make everything better when we have a problem. Most of us are surprised when there isn't a drug to fix us or a treatment to make us better—or when we find out that the information we've received is, in fact, false.

—Donatelle, *Access to Health*, 10th ed., p. 4.

_____ 1. While surveying this article, what should a skilled reader notice first?
    a. the words *pharmaceutical industry*
    b. the references to government agencies, community groups, policymakers, businesses, and health organizations
    c. the bold-faced titles and headings and the bold-faced words in the first paragraph
    d. the name of the author

_____ 2. A skilled reader might first think that this article focuses on using threats and conflict to overcome behavior changes. What adjustment will the reader make after completing the survey?
   a. The reader will realize this is the correct topic.
   b. The reader will realize this article is about poor health among college students and recommended ways to treat it.
   c. The reader will understand that this article is a comparison-and-contrast article about problems with advertising.
   d. The reader will realize that the focus of this article is on growing health issues and concerns that affect everyone.

_____ 3. All of the following questions will help the skilled reader focus on the main ideas of this article *except:*
   a. What are some of the major threats to health?
   b. How does advertising affect our health?
   c. Which pharmaceutical companies are unreliable?
   d. How can conflicting information affect our health?

_____ 4. This article suggests that
   a. everyone is at risk for diabetes.
   b. health fads do not always provide healthy advice.
   c. health issues are dying out with new technology.
   d. eating a combination of carbs and fats is the most common reason for chronic health problems.

_____ 5. Upon examining the way *chronic* is used in paragraph 1, a skilled reader should infer that a *chronic disease is* a
   a. dangerous alcoholic drink.
   b. harmful combination of things that cause obesity.
   c. persistent illness.
   d. contaminating pollutant.

_____ 6. What is the most likely definition of *touting* in paragraph 2?
   a. promoting
   b. criticizing
   c. summarizing
   d. examining

_____ 7. The word *regimens* in paragraph 2 most likely means
   a. diets.
   b. medicines.
   c. health supplements.
   d. training programs.

_____ 8. What logical conclusion can the skilled reader make about advertisements for good health from this article?
   a. These advertisements are not always reliable.
   b. These advertisements are regulated by government regulations.
   c. These advertisements offer products that are tested rigorously.
   d. These advertisements are always false.

7

_____ 9. What logical conclusion can the skilled reader make from the information in paragraph 3?
   a. Information about good health should always be trusted.
   b. The government guarantees that health industries will protect us.
   c. Information about good health is sometimes contradictory and confusing.
   d. The pharmaceutical industry has a pill for every problem.

_____ 10. Which sentence best summarizes the main ideas of this selection?
   a. Health organizations need to focus on the spread of new infectious diseases.
   b. Amidst the widespread focus on health problems is a concern about misinformation and products or advertisements that promote quick fixes.
   c. Obesity and diabetes are two of the fastest growing threats to good health, and government officials should focus on cures for these problems.
   d. Health fads should be closely assessed before they are promoted to the public.

Name _____ Section _____ Date _____ Score (number correct) _____ x 10 = _____

Directions: Read the passage and answer the questions that follow.

Conversational Problems: Prevention and Repair

Let's say, for example, that you fear your listeners will at first think a comment you're about to make is inappropriate, that they may rush to judge you without hearing your full account or that they will think you're not in full possession of your faculties ("Are you crazy?"). In these cases, you may use some form of disclaimer. A **disclaimer** is a statement that aims to ensure that your message will be understood and will not reflect negatively on you. There are several types of disclaimer.

Hedging helps you to separate yourself from the message so that if your listener rejects your message, they need not reject you (for example, "I may be wrong here, but . . ."). If a hedge is seen as indicating a lack of certainty because of some inadequacy, it will decrease the attractiveness of both women and men. However, it will be more positively received if it is seen as an indication that no one can know all about the particular subject.

Credentialing helps you establish your special qualification for saying what you're about to say ("Don't get me wrong, I'm not prejudiced.") *Sin licenses* ask listeners for permission to deviate in some way from some normally accepted practice ("I know this may not be the place to discuss business, but . . ."). *Cognitive disclaimers* help you make the case that you're in full possession of your faculties ("I know you'll think I'm crazy, but let me explain the logic of the case").

—Adapted from DeVito, *The Interpersonal Communication Book*, 12th ed., pp. 201–201.

_____ 1. Which question would a skilled reader ask while reading this passage?
    a. How might conversational problems be prevented?
    b. Who are the experts concerning conversational problems?
    c. Why do listeners have difficulty understanding some speakers?
    d. What are the advantages of being able to speak effectively in public?

_____ 2. What prior knowledge would be helpful in understanding this passage?
    a. knowledge of Latin
    b. an understanding of the fundamentals of public speaking
    c. background information about famous public speakers
    d. an understanding of the vocabulary used in discussing communication

_____ 3. What is the topic of this passage?
    a. overcoming personal disasters
    b. preventing conversational problems
    c. initiating conversation with strangers
    d. correcting misunderstandings in conversation

_____4. What is your purpose for reading this passage?
   a. to discover new ways to begin conversations
   b. to be amused by an entertaining story about conversational disasters
   c. to learn about several types of disclaimer
   d. to discover the steps to developing a speech

_____5. Upon surveying this passage, what does the skilled reader first notice?
   a. the examples buried in the passage
   b. the definitions of the italicized words and phrases
   c. The title hints at the central idea of the passage, but more information is needed.
   d. the title, the word **disclaimer**, and the words and phrases in italics

_____6. Based upon the information in the paragraph, what is the best definition for the word *disclaimer?*
   a. a statement that denies knowledge of or connection to something
   b. a statement that will help to prevent misunderstanding
   c. a provision that gives legal protection
   d. a waiver of obligation

_____7. How many types of disclaimer are discussed in the passage?
   a. one
   b. two
   c. four
   d. five

_____8. Upon examining the example in the second paragraph, what conclusion can the reader draw about *hedging*?
   a. hedging can be either a positive or negative influence
   b. hedging should never be used
   c. hedging always indicates a weakness
   d. hedging will give the speaker an unattractive appearance

_____9. According to the information in the last paragraph, the word *faculties* most likely pertains to _____.
   a. teaching staff
   b. physical abilities
   c. mental abilities
   d. psychic powers

_____10. Which of the following information will most likely follow this passage?
   a. information about chain e-mails
   b. information about excuses and apologies
   c. information about cultural sensitivity
   d. information about ethics in communication

Chapter 1: A Reading System for Skilled Readers
LAB 1.5 MASTERY TEST 1

Name _____ Section _____ Date _____ Score (number correct) _____ x 10 = _____

Directions: Read the passage and answer the questions that follow.

Benefits of Personal Finance

1 Personal finance (also referred to as **personal financial planning)** is the process of planning your spending, financing, and investing to optimize your financial situation. A **personal financial plan** specifies your financial goals and describes the spending, financing, and investing plans that are intended to achieve those goals. Although the United States is one of the wealthiest countries, many Americans do not manage their financial situations well. Consequently, they tend to rely too much on credit and have excessive debt. Consider these statistics:
- More than 1.6 million people filed for personal bankruptcy in 2004.
- The level of savings in the U.S. is only about 2 percent of income earned.
- About half of all surveyed people in the United States who are working full-time state that they live from one paycheck to the next, without a plan for saving money.
- About 40 percent of people who work full-time do not save for retirement. Those who do typically save a relatively small amount of money.

2 The lack of savings is especially problematic given the increasing cost of health care and other necessities. You will have numerous options regarding the choice of bank deposits, credit cards, loans, insurance policies, investments, and retirement plans. With an understanding of personal finance, you will be able to make decisions that can enhance your financial situation. An understanding of personal finance is beneficial to you in many ways, including the following:

Make Your Own Financial Decisions
3 An understanding of personal finance enables you to make informed decisions about your financial situation. Each of your spending decisions has an **opportunity cost,** which represents what you give up as a result of that decision. By spending money for a specific purpose, you forgo alternative ways that you could have spent the money and also forgo saving the money for a future purpose. For example, if your decision to use your cell phone costs $100 per month, you have forgone the possibility of using that money to buy concert tickets or to save for a new car. Informed financial decisions increase the amount of money that you accumulate over time and give you more flexibility to purchase the products and services you want in the future.

Judge the Advice of Financial Advisors
4 The personal financial planning process will enable you to make informed decisions about your spending, saving, financing, and investing. Nevertheless, you may prefer to rely on advice from various types of financial advisors. An understanding of personal finance allows you to judge the guidance of financial advisors and to determine whether their advice is in your best interest (or in their best interest).

——Adapted from Madura, *Personal Finance,* 3rd ed., p. 2.

11

_____ 1. Which question would a skilled reader ask while previewing this passage?
   a. Who are the best financial advisors?
   b. Which financial companies are the largest?
   c. What do I already know about personal finance?
   d. Who are the most notable bank presidents?

_____ 2. Which question would be helpful for a skilled reader to consider while reading this passage?
   a. How can an understanding of personal finance be beneficial?
   b. How many financial companies are there in the United States?
   c. What problems do most people have with money?
   d. What are the best cell phone plans that are currently available?

_____ 3. Which question should a skilled reader ask while reading the third paragraph?
   a. What is a personal financial plan?
   b. How reliable are financial advisors?
   c. What stocks will improve the most over the next few years?
   d. How can a person make good financial decisions?

_____ 4. According to the context of paragraph 1, the best definition of *finance* is
   a. the management of money.
   b. to provide money for others.
   c. money to fund a project.
   d. the amount of money someone possesses.

_____ 5. According to the context of paragraph 1, the best definition of *optimize* is
   a. have a positive outlook.
   b. write concisely.
   c. use to the best advantage.
   d. inspiring enthusiasm.

_____ 6. According to the context of paragraph 1, the best definition of *excessive* is
   a. reasonable.
   b. normal.
   c. too much.
   d. moderate.

_____ 7. Which of the following would a skilled reader highlight in this passage?
   a. the entire first paragraph
   b. the bulleted information in the first paragraph
   c. the bold-faced words and their definitions
   d. all of the last paragraph

_____ 8. Which is the best definition of an *opportunity cost*?
   a. the cost of entertainment
   b. what is lost as a result of a financial decision
   c. the price connected with job-hunting expenses
   d. the budget for marketing and business development

_____ 9. From this article, the skilled reader could assume that
   a. most people who work full time will have enough money saved for retirement.
   b. not all financial advisors give advice that is in the client's best interest.
   c. bankruptcy rates are decreasing.
   d. health-care costs are at an all-time low.

_____ 10. Which sentence best summarizes this article?
   a. People are drowning in excessive credit-card debt.
   b. Retirement plans are critical since people are staying healthier and living longer.
   c. An understanding of personal finance will be beneficial in many ways.
   d. There are many types of financial advisors.

Name _____ Section _____ Date _____ Score (number correct) _____ x 10 = _____

Directions: Read the complete sociology section and answer the questions that follow.

Making Repairs

1 At times you may say the wrong thing; then, because you can't erase the message (communication really is irreversible), you may try to account for it. Perhaps the most common method for doing so is the excuse. You learn early in life that when you do something that others will view negatively, an excuse is in order to justify your performance. Excuses, central to all forms of communication and interaction, are "explanations or actions that lessen the negative implications of an actor's performance, thereby maintaining a positive image for oneself and others."

2 Excuses seem especially in order when you say or are accused of saying something that runs counter to what is expected, or considered "right" by the people with whom you're talking. Ideally, the excuse lessens the negative impact of the message.

Some Motives for Excuse-Making

3 The major motive for excuse-making seems to be to maintain your self-esteem, to project a positive image to yourself and to others. Excuses also represent an effort to reduce stress: You may feel that if you can offer an excuse—especially a good one that is accepted by those around you—it will reduce the negative reaction and the subsequent stress that accompanies a poor performance.

4 Excuses also may enable you to maintain effective interpersonal relationships even after some negative behavior. For example, after criticizing a friend's behavior and observing the negative reaction to your criticism, you might offer an excuse such as, "Please forgive me; I'm really exhausted. I'm just not thinking straight." Excuses enable you to place your messages—even your possible failures—in a more favorable light.

Types of Excuses

Think of the recent excuses you have used or heard. Did they fall into any of these three classes?

- *I didn't do it:* Here you deny that you have done what you're being accused of doing. You may then bring up an alibi to prove you couldn't have done it, or perhaps you may accuse another person of doing what you're being blamed for doing ("I never said that" or "I wasn't even near the place when it happened"). These "I didn't do it" types are the worst excuses, because they fail to acknowledge responsibility and offer no assurance that this failure will not happen again.

- *It wasn't so bad:* Here you admit to doing it but claim the offense was not really so bad or perhaps that there was justification for the behavior ("I only padded the expense account, and even then only modestly" or "Sure, I hit him, but he was asking for it").

- *Yes, but:* Here you claim that extenuating circumstances accounted for the behavior; for example, that you weren't in control of yourself at the time or that you didn't intend to do what you did ("It was the liquor talking" or "I never intended to hurt him; I was actually trying to help").

Good and Bad Excuses

The most important question for most people is what makes a good excuse and what makes a bad excuse. How can you make good excuses and thus get out of problems, and how can you avoid bad excuses that only make matters worse? Good excuse makers use excuses in moderation; bad excuse makers rely on excuses too often. Good excuse makers avoid blaming others, especially those with whom they work; bad excuse makers blame even their work colleagues. In a similar way, good excuse makers don't attribute their failure to others or to the company; bad excuse makers do. Good excuse makers acknowledge their own responsibility for the failure by noting that they did something wrong (not that they lack competence); bad excuse makers refuse to accept any responsibility for their failures. Excuse makers who accept responsibility will be perceived as more credible, competent, and likable than those who deny responsibility.

—Adapted from DeVito, *The Interpersonal Communication Book*, 11th ed., pp. 210–211.

____ 1. Upon reading the title, the reader might first assume this article is information about making home repairs. After surveying the passage, however, the skilled reader will realize this article is about
   a. positive and negative images.
   b. moral and immoral actions.
   c. one's sense of right and wrong.
   d. making excuses.

____ 2. After surveying the title, headings, and first paragraph, which would a skilled reader anticipate to follow?
   a. a humorous story involving children and excuses
   b. the history of conversation and how it has changed over time
   c. reasons for excuses and an explanation of good and bad excuses
   d. a comparison of good and bad people

____ 3. Questions which a student might form after surveying and before reading this passage would include all of the following *except:*
   a. Why do people make excuses?
   b. How can broken marriages be repaired?
   c. What are the types of excuses?
   d. What is the difference between good excuses and bad excuses?

____ 4. According to the context of paragraph 1, the best definition of *irreversible* is
   a. permanent.
   b. important.
   c. temporary.
   d. optional.

____ 5. According to the information in this passage, the worst excuse is
   a. *I didn't do it.*
   b. *It wasn't so bad.*
   c. *Yes, but.*
   d. None of the excuses are any worse than the others. They are all equally bad.

_____ 6. According to information in this passage, if you use the excuse, "*It wasn't so bad,*" you are
   a. affirming that you will not make the same mistake again.
   b. acknowledging there was no justification for the behavior.
   c. denying that you did something wrong.
   d. claiming responsibility for the failure.

_____ 7. According to the information in paragraph 6, excuse makers may still be viewed as credible and competent people if
   a. they blame their work colleagues for their failures.
   b. they refuse to accept responsibility for their failures.
   c. they accept responsibility for their failures.
   d. they use excuses often to justify their failures.

_____ 8. The most common reason why people make excuses is
   a. because they have no sense of right or wrong.
   b. to maintain their self-esteem.
   c. to fool others into viewing them as competent people.
   d. because they see themselves as victims.

_____ 9. Based on the information in paragraph 6, the skilled reader should note
   a. there is no such thing as a good excuse.
   b. excuse makers should accept responsibility for their failures.
   c. excuses should never be accepted.
   d. that excuse makers will always be viewed as untrustworthy people.

_____ 10. Which one of the following sentences best summarizes this article?
   a. Excuses are important for relieving stressful situations.
   b. Most excuses fall into three major categories.
   c. Excuse making is a natural part of communication, but people should understand how to make excuses in a good way.
   d. The concept of a good excuse is a fallacy—nothing will excuse poor behavior.

Chapter 2: Vocabulary in Context
LAB 2.1 PRACTICE EXERCISE 1

Name _____ Section _____ Date _____ Score (number correct) _____ x 10 = _____

Objective: To determine the meanings of unfamiliar words by using context clues.

Directions: Answer the following questions by selecting the best definition of the word in boldfaced print.

____ 1. The **clamor** of the protestors was so loud that the newscasters had difficulty broadcasting their report.
   a. loud noise
   b. long speeches
   c. questions
   d. background music

____ 2. The family chose the puppy with a **docile** (quiet) nature rather than the puppy that was jumping and frantically barking for attention.
   a. curious
   b. whimsical
   c. easy to control
   d. aggressive

____ 3. The oil company tried to pin the blame for the spill on the equipment manufacturers, instead of working to **rectify** the problem.
   a. pay for
   b. sue
   c. diagnose
   d. fix

____ 4. The publisher's rejection of her novel only strengthened Carla's **resolve** to see her children's stories featured in book stores around the country.
   a. determination
   b. promotion
   c. ability
   d. requirement

____ 5. Well water from rural areas is sometimes more pure and better tasting than **municipal** water.
   a. city
   b. beauty
   c. isolation
   d. vision

____ 6. Generations ago most jobs required physical labor, whereas today many jobs are now **sedentary**.
   a. technical in nature
   b. usually involving sitting
   c. industrial
   d. overseas

____ 7. The policeman investigating the accident wanted only the important details, not the **extraneous** information about the concert the college students had planned to attend.
   a. pertinent
   b. irrelevant
   c. interesting
   d. essential

____ 8. Our society often **ostracizes** overweight people, many of whom even face job discrimination.
   a. blames
   b. ridicules
   c. ignores
   d. excludes

17

___ 9. A moderate exercise plan that includes walking every day is often more **sustainable** than fewer intense workout sessions that involve long periods of aerobic exercise and jogging.
   a. able to be maintained   b. exploiting
   c. harmless   d. exhausting

___ 10. Many desperate immigrants face a **perilous** journey in overcrowded and flimsy boats in order to reach a country where they can live in peace and be free from war.
   a. privileged   b. exciting
   c. dangerous   d. adventurous

Chapter 2: Vocabulary in Context
LAB 2.2 PRACTICE EXERCISE 2

Name _____ Section _____ Date _____ Score (number correct) _____ x 10 = _____

Objective: To determine the definitions of unfamiliar words by applying context clues.

Directions: Answer each of the following questions by selecting the best definition for the word in boldfaced print.

_____ 1. The governor's commission will conduct a **probe** into possible unlawful actions by staff members.
- a. problem
- b. examination
- c. possibility
- d. story

_____ 2. Someday developers will realize the **folly** of building massive, expensive vacation homes along hurricane-plagued beaches.
- a. foolishness
- b. seriousness
- c. success
- d. reason

_____ 3. It seemed **inevitable** that Josh would be exhausted since he was taking 16 hours of academic credit and practicing six hours a day for the swim team.
- a. capable
- b. difficult to accept
- c. bound to happen
- d. unlikely

_____ 4. Nina decided not to let others determine her fate; instead, she created her own **destiny** through hard work, diligent studying, and excellent attendance.
- a. decision and judgment
- b. answer
- c. natural talent
- d. outcome; fortune

_____ 5. After working for three weeks on his research paper, Jonathan tried to refrain from **boasting** when he received an A on the paper.
- a. brag about
- b. challenge shyly
- c. claim without confidence
- d. fail to admit

_____ 6. Although there was no visible **puncture** in the children's float, the mother searched carefully again around the sound of escaping air.
- a. expands on
- b. swelling
- c. hole
- d. decrease

_____ 7. Pessimists have an outlook of tragic **doom** when considering the future, but optimists envision positive possibilities.
- a. hopeful destiny
- b. longing for a good outcome
- c. disaster
- d. shelter

19

_____ 8. The inspirational speaker riveted the audience, and the **ensuing** applause was deafening.
a. earlier
b. happening at a previous time
c. happening at the same time
d. next; following

_____ 9. With an air of **sophistication**, the famous golfer waved at the fans.
a. refined style
b. wealth and laziness
c. selfishness
d. awkwardness

___ 10. The high school quarterback was under the **delusion** that the college scholarship would not require him to work on his academics as well as practice his talent as a wide receiver.
a. observation
b. scientific method
c. false belief
d. fact presented

Chapter 2: Vocabulary in Context
LAB 2.3 REVIEW TEST 1

Name _____ Section _____ Date _____ Score (number correct) _____ x 10 = _____

Directions: Answer each of the following questions by selecting the best definition for the word in boldfaced print.

____ 1. After Anthony was insulted by a stranger, he **retorted,** or replied wittily, to her and drew laughter from other customers in the mall.
   a. relied on intelligence
   b. replied in a sharp or witty way
   c. ignored in order to avoid arguments
   d. consulted for advice

____ 2. Obviously very different, the first brother was outgoing and **loquacious**, but the second was shy and silent.
   a. wise   c. angry
   b. shy   d. talkative

____ 3. My grandfather enjoyed the time I worked on a family history project because it gave him a chance to **reminisce** about his experiences, including those as a band member in high school, a pilot in world War II, and his job in the NASA space program.
   a. avoid discussing
   b. change
   c. make less noticeable
   d. remember

____ 4. The Senate hearing committee demanded that the corporation's officers provide **credible**— believable—documents to explain their unusual accounting procedures.
   a. practical   c. believable
   b. praiseworthy   d. worthless

____ 5. Sung was fascinated with the lectures and worked hard on his homework, unlike his classmate Ami, who seemed **indifferent** to everything, rarely participated in group discussions, and showed little interest in the readings.
   a. taking chances
   b. unresponsive and uninterested
   c. working equally but differently
   d. happening at the same time

____ 6. One might experience **awe** when in the presence of a famous and much-admired athlete, a well-known writer, or a powerful world leader.
   a. a lack of emotion
   b. pity
   c. disappointment
   d. great respect

21

_____ 7. Osama bin Laden is **infamous**—that is, has a terrible reputation throughout the Western world—for his role in the attack on the World Trade Center on September 11, 2001.
   a. popular
   b. not well known
   c. having a bad reputation
   d. accepted

_____ 8. When Alicia parked her car in the morning, she was unconcerned about her surroundings, yet at night, she became **wary** as she proceeded to the dark, isolated lot.
   a. tired
   b. cautious
   c. thin and awkward
   d. careless

_____ 9. To save money, one might adopt more **frugal** practices, including reusing plastic bags, buying items on sale, packing a lunch instead of eating fast food each day, and renting movies instead of going out on weekends.
   a. costly
   b. economical
   c. expensive
   d. boring

_____ 10. **Vital** to every human's sense of well-being are love, respect, and the opportunity to do meaningful work.
   a. related to friendship
   b. necessary
   c. not needed
   d. seeking advice

Chapter 2: Vocabulary in Context
LAB 2.4 REVIEW TEST 2

Name _____ Section _____ Date _____ Score (number correct) _____ x 10 = _____

Directions: Answer each of the following questions by selecting the best definition for the word in boldfaced print.

_____ 1. Justin proclaimed, "I have never been more **unequivocal** or firm about my innocence."
    a. unwavering   b. vague   c. angry   d. humble

_____ 2. Identify the context clue used in sentence 1.
    a. synonym   b. antonym   c. general sense   d. example

_____ 3. Mandy was **fascinating**, unlike her boring boyfriend, George.
    a. beautiful   b. sweet   c. interesting   d. loud

_____ 4. Identify the context clued used in sentence 3.
    a. synonym   b. antonym   c. general sense   d. example

_____ 5. Always trying to sell us something we don't even want, **solicitors** interrupt our dinner every evening with their phone calls.
    a. charity workers   b. sales people   c. unplanned   d. annoying operators

_____ 6. Identify the context clued used in sentence 5.
    a. synonym   b. antonym   c. general sense   d. example

_____ 7. Your **schema** about an idea includes all the memories, emotions, and experiences you bring to the idea.
    a. reading quickly   b. restatement
    c. previewed   d. way of thinking

_____ 8. **Skimming**, unlike slowly reading word for word, is an effective step to take before studying.
    a. reading quickly   b. restatement
    c. previewed   d. way of thinking

_____ 9. Amanda **surveyed** the chapter by skimming bold and italic print, studying graphics, reading their captions, thinking about what she already knew, and asking herself what she should remember.
    a. reading quickly   b. restatement
    c. previewed   d. way of thinking

_____ 10. Writing a **summary** or review of the most important ideas is a useful step to take after reading.
    a. reading quickly   b. restatement
    c. previewed   d. way of thinking

Chapter 2: Vocabulary in Context
LAB 2.5 MASTERY TEST 1

Name _____ Section _____ Date _____ Score (number correct) _____ x 10 = _____

Directions: Answer each of the following questions by selecting the best definition for the word in **bold** print.

_____ 1. Ivan and Krista were accused of cheating because their wrong answers **coincided** with each other's; for example, they both missed the same answers on their English quiz, and they used the same wording in their take-home essay.
 a. differed   b. respected   c. matched   d. concluded

_____ 2. Joe often made **disastrous** decisions, such as choosing to sell drugs and skipping out on the bail bond his family posted.
 a. wise   b. forced   c. informed   d. terrible

_____ 3. Margarita's honesty, hard work, and cooperation **inferred** or suggested that she was a person of high character.
 a. implied   b. stated   c. explained   d. denied

_____ 4. Jeremy walked at a **languid** or unhurried pace.
 a. measured   b. awkward   c. quick   d. slow

_____ 5. For many people, money is a **secondary** or minor reason they choose their careers.
 a. priority   b. significant   c. less important   d. small

_____ 6. Michael **constantly** (not just sometimes) complains about being tired.
 a. occasionally   b. never   c. always   d. lately

_____ 7. Roxy, a large dog even for a German shepherd, is not at all **aggressive** but is actually very friendly.
 a. hostile   b. calm   c. stupid   d. afraid

_____ 8. Mother showed her **frustration** when she snapped at me in a sharp tone of voice.
 a. joy   b. patience   c. irritation   d. concern

_____ 9. John walked so **briskly** that he could feel his heart race with the effort.
 a. slowly   b. quickly   c. painfully   d. purposefully

_____ 10. Jean looked forward with great **anticipation** to her boyfriend's phone call. She checked her watch every few minutes and talked excitedly about how much she wanted to hear from him.
 a. eagerness   b. fear   c. guilt   d. calm

24

Chapter 2: Vocabulary in Context
LAB 2.6 MASTERY TEST 2

Name _____ Section _____ Date _____ Score (number correct) _____ x 10 = _____

Directions: Answer each of the following questions by selecting the best definition for the word in boldfaced print.

_____ 1. Dogs barking, jets flying overhead at low altitude, and engines revving loudly are all examples of annoying **audible** sounds that destroy the peaceful atmosphere of a neighborhood.
    a. able to be heard   c. able to be avoided
    b. able to be seen   d. able to be enjoyed

_____ 2. To **illuminate** the night on the Fourth of July, our friends used sparklers and handheld candles.
    a. light up   c. create
    b. eliminate   d. make quiet

_____ 3. The coach observed his team's **bizarre** behavior (odd actions such as slurring their speech, making unnecessary fumbles, and trying to run on wobbly knees) and concluded that the players were suffering from dehydration.
    a. unusual   c. appropriate
    b. a flea market and bake sale   d. ordinary

_____ 4. College students must often face **obstacles** such as meeting financial obligations, juggling time between a part-time job and large amounts of homework, and learning new technology.
    a. work   c. difficult barrier
    b. recreational activity   d. dead end

_____ 5. Santos knew that the reading class would improve his vocabulary and comprehension, thus increasing his chances of success in **subsequent** college courses (classes in the following semesters).
    a. following   c. out of order
    b. first   d. less important

_____ 6. A student of **contemporary**, or modern, art must also study the classic works of artists from the past, recognizing that these masters produced the modern art of their own time.
    a. religious   c. not having to do with religion
    b. modern   d. former

_____ 7. We **savored** the evening, which was filled with good music, excellent food, and interesting conversation.
    a. disliked   c. enjoyed
    b. ate quickly   d. ended

_____ 8. Angela was a **compliant** daughter, unlike her brother Ben, who stubbornly challenged his parents at every opportunity.
    a. stubborn   c. challenging
    b. obedient   d. talented

Directions: Use the context clues in the following passage to determine the best meaning of the words in bold.

When research manuscripts are submitted to most journals, they undergo a process of **peer review**. Each manuscript is typically sent to two to five experts in the field. Those experts provide detailed analyses of the manuscript's rationale, methodology, and results. Only when those experts have been sufficiently satisfied do manuscripts become journal articles. This is a rigorous process, and the reviewers are quite **scrupulous** in making sure that some worthy research projects are not overlooked or that poor ones do not slip though the evaluation.

           —Adapted from Gerrig and Zimbardo, *Psychology and Life,* 18th ed., p. 43.

_____ 9. The best definition of *peer review* is _____.
    a. discussion of the good and bad points of an article
    b. examination by colleagues who are an expert in the field
    c. a summary of an article by a professor in the field
    d. a critical inspection by a higher court of law

_____ 10. The best definition of *scrupulous* is _____.
    a. simple   c. effortless
    b. controversial   d. careful

Chapter 3: Vocabulary-Building Skills
LAB 3.1 PRACTICE EXERCISE 1

Name _____ Section _____ Date _____ Score (number correct) _____ x 10 = _____

Objective: To use the glossary and context clues to determine meanings of words.

Directions: Use the glossary and the context clues to answer the following questions. Mark each sentence as true or false.

Glossary

Cholesterol	A white crystalline substance found in animal tissues and various foods
Famine	A severe food shortage that causes starvation and death in a large portion of a population in a region
Kwashiorkor	Childhood disease due to protein deprivation
Marasmus	A form of malnutrition seen in children and resulting form grossly inadequate intakes of protein, carbohydrates, fats, and micronutrients
Protein	Large, complex molecules made up of amino acids and found as essential components of all living cells.
Protein deficiency	An inadequate amount of protein
Nutrients	Chemicals found in food that are critical to human growth and function
Starches	A polysaccharide stored in plants; the storage form of glucose in plants
Vegetarians	People who restrict their diets to food substances of plant origin
Weaned	No longer taking nourishment from mother's milk

Consuming adequate **protein** is a major concern for many people. In fact, one of the most common concerns among athletes is that their diets are deficient in protein. In developed nations, this concern about dietary protein is generally unnecessary, as we can easily consume the protein our bodies need by eating an adequate amount of various foods. In contrast, people in developing nations are at risk for **protein deficiency**. A severe protein deficit in children, called **hwashiorkor**, commonly develops when a toddler is **weaned** from breast milk and fed a diet inadequate in protein and high in diluted **starches**. **Marasmus** is a disease resulting from severe deficits of all of the energy **nutrients**, as during times of **famine**.

On the other hand, too much dietary protein can be harmful. High protein intake may increase the risk of health problems. High-protein diets composed of predominantly animal sources are associated with higher blood **cholesterol** levels. This is probably due to the saturated fat in animal products, which is known to increase blood cholesterol levels and the risk of heart disease. **Vegetarians** have been shown to have a greatly reduced risk of heart disease.

—Adapted from Thompson and Manore, *Nutrition for Life,* 2nd ed., p.139, 141.

27

Directions: Read each sentence and mark the statement that follows as True or False.

_____ 1. Protein consumption is an important medical concern.
a. true
b. false

_____ 2. Athletes are one of the few groups who do not need to worry about consuming protein because of their increased amount of exercise.
a. true
b false

_____ 3. Most people in the United States should be concerned about the amount of protein they consume because the majority are at risk of protein deficiency.
a. true
b. false

_____ 4. Many young children in underdeveloped nations become at risk of hwashiorkor when they stop taking nourishment from their mothers because they eat too little protein.
a. true
b. false

_____ 5. A diet consisting primarily of rice and potatoes probably doesn't have enough starches.
a. true
b. false

_____ 6. An example of a vegetarian meal is one that consists of pasta salad, corn on the cob, black beans, and strawberries for dessert.
a. true
b. false

_____ 7. A proper amount of nutrients is important for children to grow and function   normally.
a. true
b. false

_____ 8. One can never have too much protein.
a. true
b. false

_____ 9. People who often enjoy steaks, hamburgers, and other red meats probably don't have to worry about their cholesterol.
a. true
b. false

_____ 10. Marasmus is a hunger-related disease resulting from widespread famine.
a. true
b. false

Chapter 3: Vocabulary-Building Skills
LAB 3.2 PRACTICE EXERCISE 2

Name _____ Section _____ Date _____ Score (number correct) _____ x 10 = _____

Objective: To use word parts, context clues, and a dictionary to determine appropriate word choice and meaning.

A. Directions: Using the chart and the context of each sentence, select the word from the box that best fits the meaning of the sentence.

Prefix	Meaning	Root	Meaning	Suffix	Meaning
in-	not	cred	belief	-ible	able to be
bio-	life	graph	something written	-y	quality, trait
a-	not	path	feeling		
sym-	together, with			-ic	Of, relating to

incredible	biography	apathy	sympathy	sympathetic

_____ 1. Children who are autistic are often socially unresponsive and seem to have only _____ for many around them.
   a. incredible
   b. apathy
   c. sympathy
   d. sympathetic

_____ 2. The story about the golden retriever who adopted a kitten and nursed it back to health was
   a. incredible.
   b. apathy.
   c. sympathy.
   d. sympathetic.

_____ 3. The professor listened with a(n) _____ ear to the student's plight of feeling stranded while his wife was sent overseas, leaving him with a houseful of children.
   a. incredible
   b. apathy
   c. sympathy
   d. sympathetic

_____ 4. Young people often are inspired by reading a _____ about a person who overcame great odds to become educated and successful.
   a. incredible
   b. apathy
   c. sympathy
   d. biography

_____ 5. I have no _____ for the Olympic athlete who was required to return her medals after learning that she was using performance-enhancing drugs.
   a. incredible
   b. apathy
   c. sympathy
   d. sympathetic

29

B. Directions: Using context clues, parts of speech, and the accompanying dictionary excerpt, identify the number of the definition for the word in boldfaced print in the sentences that follow this sample dictionary entry from www.yourdictionaary.com/wax.

wax[1] \waks\ *n*   **1.**   a plastic, dun-yellow substance secreted by bees for building cells; beeswax

2.   any plastic substance like this

3.   *[colloq]* a phonograph record

transitive verb

4.   to rub, polish, smear or treat with wax

5.   *[informal]* to make a phonograph record

wax[2] \waks\
intransitive verb

6.   grow gradually larger, more numerous, etc.; increase in strength, intensity, volume, etc.; said esp. of the visible face of the moon during the phases after the new moon. . .

7.   *[literary]* to become; grow (as in *was angry*)

8.   to speak or express oneself

—Adapted from *Webster's New World College Dictionary,* Copyright © 2005 by Wiley Publishing, Inc., Cleveland, Ohio. Used by arrangement with John Wiley & Sons, Inc.

_____ 6.   I am writing this by the light of the **waxing** moon in fear of being discovered.
   a.   definition 1   c.   definition 3
   b.   definition 2   d.   definition 6

_____ 7.   I must admit that memories of my dating years bring me great joy; but I **wax** sentimental.
   a.   definition 4   c.   definition 6
   b.   definition 5   d.   definition 8

_____ 8.   I thought of our times on the dance floor, slow-dancing to the **waxes** of the 1950s.
   a.   definition 1   c.   definition 3
   b.   definition 2   d.   definition 5

_____ 9.   I would have spent my life **waxing** floors just to relive those days.
   a.   definition 4   c.   definition 7
   b.   definition 6   d.   definition 8

_____ 10.   I hope that with my fortune, the bank accounts of several children's charities will **wax** larger upon my death.
   a.   definition 1   c.   definition 5
   b.   definition 2   d.   definition 7

30

Chapter 3: Vocabulary-Building Skills
LAB 3.3 REVIEW TEST 1

Name _____ Section_____ Date_____ Score (number correct) _____ x 10 = _____

A. Directions: Read the passage and fill in the following sentences using the glossary as well as context clues.

Glossary:

contrast ad an advertisement that compares the records and proposals of the candidates with a bias toward the sponsor

free media coverage of a candidate's campaign by the news media

negative ad advertising on behalf of a candidate that attacks the opponent's platform or character

paid media political advertisements purchased for a candidate's campaign

positive ad advertising on behalf of a candidate that stresses the candidate's qualifications, family, and issue positions without reference to the opponent

spot ad television advertisement on behalf of a candidate that is 60, 30, or 10 seconds long

The Media Campaign

What voters actually see and hear of the candidate is primarily determined by the **paid media** (such as television advertising) accompanying the campaign and the **free media** (newspaper and television coverage). The two kinds of media are fundamentally different: **Paid advertising** is completely under the control of the campaign, whereas the press is totally independent. Great care is taken in the design of the television advertising, which takes many approaches.

Positive ads stress the candidate's qualifications, family, and issue positions with no direct reference to the opponent. These are usually favored by the incumbent candidate. **Negative ads** attack the opponent's character and platform and may not even mention the candidate who is paying for their airing (except for a brief, legally required identification at the ad's conclusion). In 1996, Steve Forbes made extensive use of negative ads prior to the Iowa caucus and the New Hampshire primary, spending millions denouncing then front-runner Bob Dole. These attacks prompted Dole to tag Forbes "the king of negative advertising," before unleashing some negative ads of his own. These ads contributed to the generally held belief that the early stages of the 1996 Republican nomination battle was one of the most vicious ever witnessed. **Contrast ads** compare the records and proposals of the candidates with a bias toward the sponsor. And whether the public likes them or not, all three kinds of ads can inject important (as well as trivial) issues into a campaign.

Occasionally, advertisements are relatively long (ranging from four-and-one-half minute ads to thirty-minute documentaries). Usually, however, the messages are short **spot ads** that are 60, 30, or even 10 seconds long.

—Adapted from O'Connor and Sabato, *The Essentials of American Government,* Copyright © 1998, pp. 351–353.

_____ 1. A campaign presentation that does not mention the opponent but stresses a candidate's stand on certain issues as well as his or her qualifications is a
   a. contrast ad.   c. negative ad.
   b. positive ad.   d. spot ad.

_____ 2. An ad that lasts only ten seconds is a
   a. contrast ad.   c. negative ad.
   b. positive ad.   d. spot ad.

_____ 3. A _____ compares the records of both candidates but presents one in a more favorable light than the other.
   a. free media   c. negative ad
   b. positive ad   d. contrast ad

_____ 4. A _____ is coverage of a candidate's campaign by the news media such as newspapers and television and would most likely present the positive and negative aspects of the person.
   a. positive ad   c. free media
   b. negative ad   d. spot ad

_____ 5. The _____ might present the sponsoring candidate in a favorable light during a television commercial while criticizing the opponent's character.
   a. paid media   c. negative ad
   b. free media   d. contrast ad

B. Directions: Use the context clues and your knowledge of word parts to determine which definition corresponds to the word from the passage.

Positive ads stress the candidate's qualifications, family, and issue positions with no direct reference to the opponent. These are usually favored by the **incumbent** candidate.

_____ 6. Incumbent means
   a. cause.   c. kind.
   b. current.   d. favoritism.

In 1996 Steve Forbes made extensive use of negative ads prior to the Iowa caucus and the New Hampshire primary, spending millions **denouncing** then front-runner Bob Dole.

_____ 7. Denounce means
   a. criticize.   c. cause.
   b. cruel.   d. current.

These attacks **prompted** Dole to tag Forbes "the king of negative advertising," before unleashing some negative ads of his own.

_____ 8. Prompt means
   a. current.   c. cause.
   b. criticize.   d. kind.

These ads contributed to the generally held belief that the early stages of the 1996 Republican nomination battle was one of the most **vicious** ever witnessed.

____ 9. Vicious means
      a. kind.
      b. cruel.
      c. current.
      d. cause.

Contrast ads compare the records and proposals of the candidates with a **bias** toward the sponsor.

____ 10. Bias means
      a. cause.
      b. current.
      c. criticize.
      d. favoritism.

Chapter 3: Vocabulary-Building Skills
LAB 3.4 REVIEW TEST 2

Name _____ Section _____ Date _____ Score (number correct) _____ x 10 = _____

Directions: Using the chart and the context of each sentence, select the word that best fits the meaning of the sentence.

Prefix	Meaning	Root	Meaning	Suffix	Meaning
con-	with	tain	hold	-er, -or	thing or person
dis-	apart	spers	scatter	-al	related to
In-	intro, on	struct	build	-tion	action, state

1. The _____ of the Stephens' house is almost finished.
   a. container   b. instructor   c. construction   d. dispersal

2. When the protestors became too noisy, the police ordered their _____.
   a. container   b. instructor   c. construction   d. dispersal

3. The _____ for the iced tea is on the third shelf.
   a. container   b. instructor   c. construction   d. dispersal

4. The _____ taught the class the basic information.
   a. container   b. instructor   c. construction   d. dispersal

Directions: Examine the glossary words from a health textbook. Based on the definition of each word and the context of each sentence, label the statements that follow the list as true or false.

GLOSSARY

Heat cramps   Muscle cramps that occur during or following exercise in warm or hot weather

Heat exhaustion   A heat stress illness caused by loss of water due to exercising in warm or hot conditions. Often comes before a stroke

Heat stroke   A deadly heat stress illness resulting from loss of water and overexertion in warm or hot conditions. It can cause the body temperature to rise from normal to 105° or 110° in just a few minutes.

Hypothermia   A possibly fatal condition caused by unusually low body temperatures.

—Adapted from Donatelle, *Access to Health,* 7th ed., p. 304.

34

_____ 5. Lack of sufficient water while exercising in hot conditions can be dangerous.
    a.   true
    b.   false

_____ 6. Heat exhaustion is often linked to strokes.
    a.   true
    b.   false

_____ 7. Heat cramps can occur during or after exercise.
    a.   true
    b.   false

_____ 8. Heat stroke is not life-threatening.
    a.   true
    b.   false

_____ 9. A low body temperature often signals heat stroke.
    a.   true
    b.   false

_____ 10. Hypothermia can lead to loss of life.
    a.   true
    b.   false

Chapter 3: Vocabulary-Building Skills
LAB 3.5 MASTERY TEST 1

Name _____ Section _____ Date _____ Score (number correct) _____ x 10 = _____

A. Directions: Read the passage and fill in the sentences using the glossary as well as context clues.

GLOSSARY:

attempt	an incomplete criminal act; the closest act to the completion of the crime
concurrence	the legal requirement for a crime, that there is a union of *actus reus* and *mens rea*
elements of a crime	the illegal actions (*actus reus*) and criminal intentions (*mens rea*) of the actor along with the circumstances that link the two, especially causation
inchoate offenses	incomplete crimes such as solicitation, conspiracy, and attempt
principle of proportionality	the belief that less serious harms should carry lesser punishments than more serious harms

Punishments specified by law are based on the **principle of proportionality**. Less serious harms, such as misdemeanors, carry lesser punishment than more serious harms, which are classified as felonies. However, even within felonies there are various degrees of punishment. Determining what punishment should be attached to a crime depends on the conduct and the intention of the perpetrator. Each crime is defined by two important **elements**—*actus reus* and *mens rea.*

Consider the case of an employee who harbors ill will toward a supervisor. Assume that the employee is in danger of losing his or her job and a performance review is imminent. The employee strikes the supervisor in the parking lot with his or her automobile and causes harm. Is the action a crime or an accident? If the employee had no criminal intent at the time he or she hit the supervisor, then it is an accident. The **principle of concurrence** requires that criminal intent is present at the time of the act, such that having criminal intent prior to or following the act does not satisfy the requirement. The requirement of concurrence raises questions about incomplete crimes, in which the *actus reus* and the *mens rea* do not coincide but would have if the person had completed all he or she had planned, or if circumstances had been different.

One cannot be convicted of a crime for thinking about murder, rape, robbery, larceny, burglary, or any other crime. The law punishes people only for what they do, not what they think. Crimes that go beyond mere thought but do not result in completed crimes are called incomplete crimes or **inchoate offenses**. The three common inchoate offenses are (1) solicitation, (2) conspiracy, and (3) **attempt**. Attempt, conspiracy, and solicitation stand on a continuum, with attempt closest to and solicitation farthest from actual commission of the crime.

—Adapted from Fagin, *Criminal Justice,* 2nd ed., pp. 160, 164

____ 1. According to the **principle of proportionality**, a theft of a ten-dollar item could result in several years in prison.
    a. true
    b. false

36

_____ 2. Illegal actions and criminal intentions form the two main **elements** of a crime.
   a. true
   b. false

_____ 3. According to the **principle of concurrence**, an employee who is enraged over a demotion and injures his or her boss as a result could be arrested.
   a. true
   b. false

_____ 4. A predator who attempts to meet with a young child for sexual gratification, but does not follow through, has committed an **inchoate offense**.
   a. true
   b. false

_____ 5. **Attempt** of a crime is not considered as severe by the courts as solicitation for a crime.
   a. true
   b. false

B. Directions: Use the following sample dictionary entry to answer the statements below as true or false.

Art • less *adj*
   1. having or displaying no cunning, guile, or deceit
   2. free of artificiality; natural
   3. lacking art, knowledge, or skill; uncultured, ignorant
   4. poorly made or done; crude

_____ 6. Based on the first definition, an artless person is probably naïve or innocent of intending harm.
   a. true
   b. false

_____ 7. Based on the second definition, an artless person is an insincere person.
   a. true
   b. false

_____ 8. Based on the third definition, an artless person has little understanding of the art world.
   a. true
   b. false

_____ 9. Based on the fourth definition, a vase that is artlessly made will probably not be highly valued.
   a. true
   b. false

_____ 10. *Artful* is probably the opposite of *artless*—as in the sentence "The painting was artfully drawn."
   a. true
   b. false

Chapter 3: Vocabulary-Building Skills
Lab 3.6 MASTERY TEST 2

Name _____ Section _____ Date _____ Score (number correct) _____ x 10 = _____

Directions: Study the following words in their context. Then answer the questions that follow them.

biased
Mother is **biased** against my boyfriend just because he has his nose, tongue, and eyebrows pierced.
The lawyer carefully questioned each possible juror to find out if any of the jurors were **biased** in favor of the death penalty.

kink
It took a long time to straighten the hose because there were so many **kinks** in it.
He got a **kink** in his back after lifting the dresser and carrying it down two flights of steps.

primary
Robert's **primary** or chief worry was his wife's safety.
A **primary** (basic) education includes reading, writing, and mathematics.

sequence
You must follow the correct **sequence** of steps to process a refund on any return to this store.
The skilled writer uses a proven **sequence** of activities: think, write, and rewrite.

topic
For many students, the hardest part of writing is thinking up a **topic** or subject about which to write.
The **topic** for today's discussion is "gang violence."

Directions: Choose the correct definition of the word based upon the context.

1. Biased means _____.
   a. order
   b. main
   c. subject
   d. knot
   e. holding a one-sided point of view

2. Kink means _____.
   a. order
   b. main
   c. subject
   d. knot
   e. holding a one-sided point of view

3. Primary means _____.
   a. order
   b. main
   c. subject
   d. knot
   e. holding a one-sided point of view

4. Sequence means _____.
   a. order
   b. main
   c. subject
   d. knot
   e. holding a one-sided point of view

5. Topic means _____.
   a. order
   b. main
   c. subject
   d. knot
   e. holding a one-sided point of view

Directions: Fill in the blank with the correct word.

6. After sleeping on the sofa all night, Heather spent nearly an hour getting the _____ out of her hair.
   a. biased
   b. kinks
   c. primary
   d. sequence
   e. topic

7. Two _____ needs for human beings are food and shelter.
   a. biased
   b. kink
   c. primary
   d. sequence
   e. topic

8. What is the _____ of the article you are reading?
   a. biased
   b. kink
   c. primary
   d. sequence
   e. topic

9. For generations, women worked against the _____ belief that they should not vote or work outside the home.
   a. biased
   b. kink
   c. primary
   d. sequence
   e. topic

10. You must take your courses in their proper _____ to make sure you can build solid basic skills.
    a. biased
    b. kink
    c. primary
    d. sequence
    e. topic

Chapter 4: Topics and Main Ideas
LAB 4.1 PRACTICE EXERCISE 1

Name _____ Section _____ Date _____ Score (number correct) _____ x 10 = _____

Objective: To recognize the difference between general and specific ideas.

Directions: Choose the item that is the most general of the group.

_____ 1.
   a. computer
   b. technology
   c. keyboard
   d. backspace key

_____ 2.
   a. mortgage payments
   b. utility bills
   c. household costs
   d. high-speed Internet bill

_____ 3.
   a. hot dog cart
   b. farmer's market
   c. food vending
   d. ice cream truck

_____ 4.
   a. copperhead snake
   b. poisonous snake
   c. rattlesnake
   d. cottonmouth snake

B. Directions: Choose the main idea from each group of items.

_____ 5. Choose the main idea from the list below.
   a. The atomic bombs dropped on two cities in Japan let loose a power never seen before.
   b. A total of 130,000 people died because of the bombs.
   c. The force of each bomb was greater than 20,000 tons of dynamite.
   d. The atomic bomb

_____ 6. Choose the main idea from the list below.
   a. Many Buddhists are vegetarians.
   b. Food preferences
   c. A person's religion can influence his or her food choices.
   d. Mormons may limit their meat intake and avoid caffeinated beverages.

_____ 7. Choose the main idea from the list below.
   a. You can use several tactics to maintain a healthy diet.
   b. Avoid all-you-can-eat buffets.
   c. Choose lower-fat versions of your favorite meals.
   d. Healthy eating

_____ 8. Choose the main idea from the list below.
   a. Many Buddhists are vegetarians.
   b. Food preferences
   c. A person's religion can also influence his or her food choices.
   d. Mormons may limit their meat intake and avoid caffeinated beverages.

_____ 9. Choose the main idea from the list below.
   a. Fluoride stimulates new bone growth.
   b. Fluoride has many benefits.
   c. The trace mineral fluoride
   d. Fluoride combines with calcium to make teeth more resistant to cavities

_____ 10. Choose the main idea from the list below.
   a. Sports drinks
   b. Sports drinks help athletes consume more energy than they could by eating solid food and water.
   c. Sports beverages can benefit athletes in several ways.
   d. Athletes can train longer by drinking sports beverages.

Chapter 4: Topics and Main Ideas
LAB 4.2 PRACTICE EXERCISE 2

Name _____ Section_____ Date_____Score (number correct) _____ x 10 = _____

Directions: Read each of the following groups of ideas. Then answer the question that follows each group.

Group 1
  A. Certain activities can help increase your creativity.
  B. Join clubs where you can develop new interests.
  C. Surf the Web for new ideas.
  D. Increasing your creativity

_____ 1. Item D states
     a. the topic.
     b. the main idea.
     c. a supporting detail.
     d. a central theme.

Group 2
  A. Skin cancer is one of the most common cancers.
  B. Skin cancer is most often found in people who are often exposed to the sun.
  C. Skin cancer
  D. Every year, nearly half a million Americans are diagnosed with skin cancer.

_____ 2. Item A states
     a. the topic.
     b. the main idea.
     c. a supporting detail.
     d. a central theme.

_____ 3. Which of the following items is the topic for this group?
     a. Smiling at colleagues is considered good office etiquette.
     b. The importance of small things
     c. The wisest of people have learned the importance of doing small things.
     d. Shaking hands and repeating a person's name can make a person feel valued.

_____ 4. Which of the following ideas is the main idea?
     a. Memory tricks for students
     b. To remember the spelling of *dessert,* think of strawberry shortcake.
     c. To remember the spelling of *desert,* think of the Sahara.
     d. Students often use mnemonics, or memory tricks, to handle spelling problems.

43

B. Directions: Read each of the following paragraphs. Then answer the questions that follow.

[1]People may encounter several barriers to organizing the family's photographs. [2]First of all, it takes hours to go through and sort the stacks of images. [3]Each image brings a story to mind, and the need to talk about the memory is irresistible. [4]Second, it takes work. [5]Each photo should be labeled with the names of the people in the picture, the occasion, and the date. [6]Finally, it can be expensive to create picture albums. [7]But for people who decide to take on the task of creating their family's pictorial history, the time, effort, and money are well worth the effort.

_____ 5. What is the topic of the passage?
   a. creating a family picture album
   b. creating family history
   c. pictures
   d. hard work

_____ 6. Which sentence states the main idea?
   a. sentence 1
   b. sentence 2
   c. sentence 5
   d. sentence 7

[1]Car racing is a dangerous business, and few people succeed at it. [2]Despite his success, Jeff Gordon seems to be a humble man. [3]Gordon is one of a few men who have won the Winston Cup championship race four times. [4]Since he is only around 30 years old, if he continues as he has, he is destined to win again. [5]His hard work and skillful driving of his Chevrolet earned him nearly $6 million in 2001. [6]However, Gordon never boasts about his own abilities. [7]In every interview, he gives credit to his crew first.

_____ 7. What is the topic of the paragraph?
   a. car racing
   b. Jeff Gordon's success and humility
   c. Jeff Gordon's wins
   d. Jeff Gordon's crew

_____ 8. Which sentence states the main idea of the paragraph?
   a. sentence 1
   b. sentence 2
   c. sentence 5
   d. sentence 7

[1]A reading strategy is a way of thinking. [2]Skilled readers think about what they are reading before, during, and after reading. [3]Before you read, ask yourself what you already know about the topic. [4]Then quickly look over the passage or chapter and think about the author's purpose. [5]Also look at any pictures, charts, or graphs. [6]Now you are ready to read. [7]During reading, take time to think about topic, subtopics, and the author's main point. [8]But if you get confused, reread the last few sentences. [9]Or you can read ahead to see if more information will help you make sense of the ideas. [10]After reading, take time to think about what you have read, and ask yourself, "What did I learn?"

_____ 9. What is the topic of the paragraph?
- a. reading strategies
- b. before-reading questions
- c. after-reading questions
- d. during-reading strategies

_____ 10. Which sentence states the main idea of the paragraph?
- a. sentence 2
- b. sentence 3
- c. sentence 7
- d. sentence 10

Chapter 4: Topics and Main Ideas
LAB 4.3 REVIEW TEST 1

Name _____ Section _____ Date _____ Score (number correct) _____ x 10 = _____

Directions: Answer the following questions based upon this group of ideas.

A. The shag is a dance with a rich American history still enjoyed by thousands today.
B. The shag actually began in the 1920s and adapted to the beat of Elvis and the Beatles; today every state in the country has a shag club.
C. The shag's steps are much like the steps to the jitterbug.
D. The shag

_____ 1. The topic is found in
    a. item A.   c. item C.
    b. item B.   d. item D.

_____ 2. The main idea is found in
    a. item A.   c. item C.
    b. item B.   d. item D.

_____ 3. The first supporting detail is found in
    a. item A.   c. item C.
    b. item B.   d. item D.

_____ 4. The second supporting detail is found in
    a. item A.   c. item C.
    b. item B.   d. item D.

Directions: Read each paragraph and answer the questions that follow.

[1]The Cherokees lived freely and happily in the mountains of Virginia, West Virginia, North and South Carolina, Kentucky, Tennessee, Georgia, and Alabama. [2]Cherokees lived well because they respected order and authority. [3]The Cherokee tribe was made up of seven clans. [4]Clans are groups of people who come from the same ancestor. [5]The clans lived in small towns, and each town had its own chief and counsel. [6]Both men and women spoke at the council. [7]The Cherokees believed in balance and order; they tried to live by their beliefs so they would have good lives.

_____ 5. What is the topic of the paragraph?
    a. balance and order
    b. clans
    c. the Cherokee tribe
    d. Cherokee men and women

_____ 6. Which sentence states the main idea of the paragraph?
    a. sentence 1
    b. sentence 3
    c. sentence 6
    d. sentence 7

[1]Fannie Lou Hamer took a bold stand for equality. [2]She was born poor and black in the state of Mississippi on October 6, 1917. [3]She was the youngest of 19 children. [4]She had 14 brothers and four sisters. [5]At the time Fannie Lou was born, African Americans were still being prevented from voting, and no woman of any color could vote. [6]So when Freedom Fighters came to Mississippi in the summer of 1962 to turn the state into a place where African Americans could vote without restrictions, Fannie Lou registered to vote. [7]This courageous step caused her much trouble. [8]She was thrown off the plantation where she lived with her husband and children. [9]She was beaten and thrown in jail. [10]None of this stopped her, however. [11]Eventually, her courage and determination won her notice. [12]Her testimony about the African American struggle for equality in front of the United States Senate was a key event in the civil rights movement.

_____ 7. What is the topic of the paragraph?
  a. Mississippi
  b. the civil rights movement
  c. Fannie Lou Hamer
  d. Freedom Fighters

_____ 8. Which sentence states the main idea of the paragraph?
  a. sentence 1
  b. sentence 2
  c. sentence 5
  d. sentence 12

[1]Maya Lin, a senior at Yale University, won the competition to design the Vietnam War Memorial. [2]More than 1,400 people had applied, but the 21-year-old Chinese American art student won the $20,000 prize and her place in history. [3]Maya Lin had a definite purpose in her design for the Vietnam War Memorial. [4]First, she wanted the memorial to be made of black marble, instead of white, so that it could be polished to a high gloss. [5]She wanted a mirror-like finish that would reflect the faces of the visitors upon the names of the slain soldiers carved on its face. [6]She also insisted that the names be listed in chronological order, by the date on which the soldiers died. [7]She thought this would avoid the look of a telephone book and would also place soldiers with their units, the men and women with whom they served and died. [8]Finally, she insisted that only the names of the soldiers should be engraved on the memorial. [9]In fact, her own name appears on the back of the memorial, not on its face.

_____ 9. What is the topic of the paragraph?
  a. Chinese American artists
  b. Maya Lin
  c. Maya Lin's design of the Vietnam War Memorial
  d. the $20,0000 prize

_____ 10. Which sentence states the main idea of the paragraph?
  a. sentence 2
  b. sentence 3
  c. sentence 4
  d. sentence 9

Chapter 4: Topics and Main Ideas
Lab 4.4 REVIEW TEST 2

Name _____ Section _____ Date _____ Score (number correct) _____ x 10 = _____

Directions: Answer the following questions based upon this group of ideas.

- A. A vegetarian diet results in reduced risk for obesity, type 2 diabetes, high blood pressure, and heart disease.
- B. Many people practice vegetarianism because of its health benefits.
- C. Another health benefit of a vegetarian diet is the reduced risk of some cancers, particularly colon cancer.
- D. Vegetarian diets

_____ 1. The topic is found in
- a. item A.
- b. item B.
- c. item C.
- d. item D.

_____ 2. The main idea is found in
- a. item A.
- b. item B.
- c. item C.
- d. item D.

_____ 3. The first supporting detail is found in
- a. item A.
- b. item B.
- c. item C.
- d. item D.

_____ 4. The second supporting detail is found in
- a. item A.
- b. item B.
- c. item C.
- d. item D.

Directions: Read each paragraph and answer the questions which follow.

[1]The values of any society are reflected in various aspects of everyday life. [2]However, we can also find clues to our culture's values by looking at the "superheroes" that we celebrate. [3]Superman, for example, defines our society as good. [4]After all, Superman fights for "truth, justice, and the American way." [5]Other superheroes have stories that draw on great people in our history, including religious figures such as Moses and Jesus. [6]They are tested through great moral challenges, and they finally succeed in overcoming all obstacles.

—Adapted from Macionis, *Sociology*, 13th ed., pp. 82–83.

_____ 5. What is the topic of the paragraph?
   a. celebration of superheroes
   b. clues to everyday life
   c. Superman' challenges
   d. cultural clues provided by superheroes

_____ 6. Which sentence states the main idea of the paragraph?
   a. sentence 1
   b. sentence 2
   c. sentence 3
   d. sentence 5

[1]Sheri Springs-Phillips is a neurology resident at Loyola University Medical Center. [2]On her 11-year journey to becoming a doctor, she piled up $102,000 in debt. [3]Although her friends think she's got it made, she worries about the $2,500 monthly loan payments that begin when she finishes her residency. [4]Fortunately, Sheri is an exception, but just the average level of debt can be daunting. [5]Most graduates leave college owing a significant amount in loans and will need a solid financial plan to manage their debt. [6]Thus, a good financial plan may not help these people earn more, but it can help them use the money that they do earn to achieve their financial goals.

—Adapted from Keown, *Personal Finance: Turning Money into Wealth*, 5th ed., p. 4.

_____ 7. What is the topic of the paragraph?
   a. managing college debt
   b. financial loans
   c. college graduates
   d. Sheri Springs-Phillips' financial goals

_____ 8. Which sentence states the main idea of the paragraph?
   a. sentence 1
   b. sentence 2
   c. sentence 3
   d. sentence 6

[1]Research shows that *sprawl*, the spread of people out from urban areas, has many negative effects. [2]To some people, the word sprawl means strip malls, look-alike commercial development, and tracts of cookie-cutter houses crowding out farmland and ranchland. [3]It may suggest traffic jams, destruction of wildlife habitat, and loss of natural land around cities. [4]Sprawl's effects on transportation creates increased pollution, resulting in urban smog and, more importantly, global climate change. [5]Some research suggests that sprawl even promotes obesity because driving cars takes the place of walking during daily errands.

—Adapted from Withgott and Brennan, *Essential Environment: The Science Behind the Stories*, 3rd. ed. pp. 188–189.

_____ 9. What is the topic of the paragraph?
   a. urban problems
   b. causes of pollution
   c. effects of sprawl
   d. results of crowding

_____10. Which sentence states the main idea of the paragraph?
   a. sentence 1
   b. sentence 2
   c. sentence 3
   d. sentence 5

Chapter 4: Topics and Main Ideas
LAB 4.5 MASTERY TEST 1

Name _____ Section _____ Date _____ Score (number correct) _____ x 10 = _____

A. Directions: Answer the following questions based upon this group of ideas.

Group 1

A. Plastic surgery is often used to improve a person's looks.
B. Skin grafts replace burned or damaged skin.
C. Plastic surgery
D. One type of plastic surgery, called rhinoplasty, reduces the size of the nose.

____ 1. What is the topic?
    a. item A   c. item C
    b. item B   d. item D

____ 2. The main idea can be found in
    a. item A.   c. item C.
    b. item B.   d. item D.

Group 2

A. A person's fingerprints are just like a signature.
B. Fingerprinting
C. Fingerprint records can be used by law enforcement to identify criminals.
D. Fingerprinting is a science that uses the pattern of ridges on the fingertips to identify a person.

____ 3. The topic is found in
    a. item A.   c. item C.
    b. item B.   d. item D.

____ 4. The main idea can be found in
    a. item A.   c. item C.
    b. item B.   d. item D.

Group 3

A. Yellow journalism
B. Yellow journalism uses emotion instead of facts to sell newspapers.
C. For example, a newspaper may mislabel a picture for a shocking effect.
D. Some think that the popular *National Enquirer* uses yellow journalism

____ 5. The topic is found in
    a. item A.   c. item C.
    b. item B.   d. item D.

_____ 6. The main idea can be found in
  a. item A.   c. item C.
  b. item B.   d. item D.

B. Directions: Read each paragraph and answer the questions that follow.

[1]Children would be disoriented and bewildered were it not for what their parents tell them about the world; much of this talk has its roots in fairy tales. [2]Much of what parents say is moralistic—usually warnings about the dire consequences of disobedience. "The Three Little Pigs," for example, advises children how to plan sensibly for the future and tells them that hard work and diligence, not fun and frivolity, are what pay off in the long run. [3]Little Red Riding Hood is explicitly warned by her mother not to talk to strangers. [4]Similarly, the mother goat in "The Wolf and the Seven Kids" goes off, leaving her children home alone with the admonition not to open the door to anyone. [5]Like Red Riding Hood, most of the seven little goats pay for their disobedience by being eaten whole; of course, as often happens in fairy-tale land, they are rescued none the worse for their ordeal.

—Janaro and Altshuler, *The Art of Being Human*, 6th ed., p. 509.

_____ 7. What is the topic?
  a. the importance of learning good behavior
  b. how children learn about obedience from fairy tales as well as parents
  c. how "The Three Little Pigs" teaches children to plan ahead
  d. teaching children

_____ 8. Which sentence states the main idea of the paragraph?
  a. sentence 1   c. sentence 3
  b. sentence 2   d. sentence 5

[1]Modern interpreters of fairy tales, especially psychiatrists, point to early misconceptions and warped expectations that children derive from fairy tales. [2]The hunter will come and take care of the wicked wolf. [3]The Prince will kiss Sleeping Beauty and awaken her from her century-long slumber. Prince Charming will discover that the wretchedly dirty girl in the corner has the only foot capable of fitting the glass slipper. [4]And so, they contend, that we grow up believing that true love will find a way and that bad people always get what's coming to them.

—Janaro and Altshuler, *The Art of Being Human*, 6th ed., p. 510.

_____ 9. What is the topic?
  a. misconceptions derived from fairy tales
  b. the problem with Prince Charming
  c. interpretations of literature
  d. happy endings

_____ 10. Which sentence states the main idea of the paragraph?
  a. sentence 1
  b. sentence 2
  c. sentence 3
  d. sentence 5

52

Chapter 4: Topics and Main Ideas
LAB 4.6 MASTERY TEST 2

Name _____ Section _____ Date _____ Score (number correct) _____ x 10 = _____

A. Directions: Choose the item that is the most general of the group.

_____ 1.
    a. reference book   b. book
    c. atlas   d. *The Rand McNally Atlas*

_____ 2.
    a. illness   b. childhood disease
    c. measles   d. German measles

_____ 3.
    a. paragraph   b. essay   c. word   d. sentence

_____ 4.
    a. Fourth of July   b. patriotic holiday
    c. holiday   d. American holiday

_____ 5.
    a. Madonna   b. popular singer   c. female singer   d. singer

B. Directions: Choose the best topic of the paragraph.

Geologists use several techniques to determine the ages of rocks and the fossils they contain. The method most often used, called radiometric dating, is based on the measurement of certain radioactive isotopes (see Module 2.4). Fossils contain isotopes of elements that accumulated when the organisms were alive. For example, the carbon in a living organism includes both the most common isotope, carbon-12 (^{12}C), and a less common radioactive isotope, carbon-14 (^{14}C), in the same ratio as is present in the atmosphere.

—Campbell, Reece, Taylor, and Simon, *Biology: Concepts and Connections*,
5th ed., p. 299.

_____ 6. What is the topic of the passage?
    a. techniques to determine the ages of rocks and fossils
    b. isotopes of elements
    c. scientific techniques
    d. fossils

53

In 1999, President Clinton proposed allocating much of the new budget surplus to Social Security and investing some of it in the stock market. Social Security and Medicare account for about one-third of the federal budget. Other social service expenditures have increased in growth as well. No brief list can do justice to the range of government social programs, which provide funds for the elderly, businesses run by minority entrepreneurs, consumer education, drug rehabilitation, environmental education, food subsidies for the poor, guaranteed loans to college students, housing allowances for the poor, inspections of hospitals, and so on. Consequently, it can be seen that the rise of a social service state has contributed enormously to America's growing budget.

—Adapted from Edwards, Wattenberg, and Lineberry, *Government in America: People, Politics, and Policy,* 12th ed., p. 451.

_____ 7. What is the topic of the passage?
a. President Clinton's budget proposal
b. the rising cost of Medicare
c. the impact of social services on the federal budget
d. government programs

The People's Republic of China is the world's most populous nation, home to one-fifth of the 6.7 billion people living on Earth at the start of 2008. When Mao Ze Tung founded the country's current regime 59 years ago, he believed that population growth was desirable. Under his leadership, China grew and changed. The population began to swell, and at that time, the average Chinese woman gave birth to 5.8 children. Unfortunately, the country's population was eroding the nation's soils, depleting its water, leveling its forest, and polluting its air. Chinese leaders realized that the nation might not be able to feed its people if their numbers grew much larger. Thus, the government decided to institute a population-control program stipulating that Chinese couples could have only one child.

—Adapted from Withgott and Brennan, *Environment: The Science Behind the Stories*, 3rd ed., p. 207.

_____ 8. What is the topic of the passage?
a. The People's Republic of China
b. China's ecological problems
c. the impact of social services on the federal budget
d. China's one-child program

Conflict can have several positive effects. Among the advantages of conflict is that it forces you to examine a problem and work toward a potential solution. If you use productive conflict strategies, your relationship is likely to become stronger, healthier, and more satisfying than it was before. Conflict often prevents hostilities and resentments from festering. Say you're annoyed at your partner, who comes home from work and then talks on the phone with colleagues for two hours instead of giving that time to you. If you say nothing, your annoyance is likely to grow. Further, by saying nothing you implicitly approve of such behavior, so it's likely that the phone calls will continue and your relationship will deteriorate even more.

—Adapted from DeVito, *The Interpersonal Communication Book*, 11th ed. p. 288.

_____ 9. What is the topic of the passage?
   a. The buildup of hostility and resentment in a partnership
   b. Potential solutions to problems
   c. Annoying behavior
   d. Positive effects of conflict

You may agree that the end of a relationship, an earthquake, or prejudice might cause stress, but what about the smaller stressors you experience on a day-to-day basis? What happened to you yesterday? You probably didn't get a divorce or survive a plane crash. You're more likely to have lost your notes or textbook. Perhaps you were late for an important appointment, or you got a parking ticket, or a noisy neighbor ruined your sleep. These are the types of recurring day-to-day stressors that confront most people, most of the time.

—Adapted from Gerrig and Zimbardo, *Psychology and Life,* 18th ed., p. 396.

_____ 10. What is the topic of the passage?
   a. Major reasons for stress
   b. Day-to-day stressors
   c. Catastrophes
   d. Daily living

Chapter 5: Locating Stated Main Ideas
LAB 5.1 PRACTICE EXERCISE 1

Name _____ Section _____ Date _____ Score (number correct) _____ x 10 = _____

Objective: To identify the main idea in a paragraph by considering the supporting details.

Directions: Identify the topic sentence of each paragraph.

1 [1]In the last few decades, a serious issue concerning immunizations has emerged. [2]Parents of young children have begun to resist getting their infants and young children immunized against childhood diseases, such as measles, mumps, and rubella, probably due to a number of factors. [3]First, the parents of these children have grown up in an era in which immunizations during infancy were common, making them unaware of the seriousness of the childhood diseases those immunizations prevent. [4]Second, many of these parents have become influenced by misinformation that has been placed on the Internet and handed out by concerned but uninformed people that highlights the dangers of immunization.

—Adapted from Ciccarelli and White, *Psychology*, 2nd ed., p.324.

_____ 1. Which sentence is the topic sentence of the paragraph?
      a.   sentence 1   b.   sentence 2
      c.   sentence 3   d.   sentence 4

2 [1]A rookie in professional baseball may feel self-conscious during the first few games in the big leagues but go on to develop a comfortable sense of fitting in with the team. [2]Coming to feel at home on the field was slow and painful for Jackie Robinson. [3]Robinson knew that many white players, and millions of white fans, resented his presence. [4]In time, however, his outstanding ability and his confident and cooperative manner won him the respect of the entire nation.

—Adapted from Macionis, *Sociology*, 13th ed., p. 20.

_____ 2. Which sentence is the topic sentence of the paragraph?
      a.   sentence 1   b.   sentence 2
      c.   sentence 3   d.   sentence 4

3 [1]Just as dams on rivers use flowing fresh water to generate hydroelectric power, some scientists, engineers, businesses, and governments are developing ways to use kinetic energy from the motion of ocean water to generate electrical power. [2]The rise and fall of ocean tides twice each day moves large amounts of water past any given point on the world's coastlines. [3]Tides are especially strong in long, narrow bays such as Alaska's Cook Inlet or the Bay of Fundy between New Brunswick and Nova Scotia. [4]Such locations are best for harnessing tidal energy by erecting dams across the outlets of tidal basins. [5]As tidal currents pass through the dam, water turns turbines to generate electricity.

—Adapted from Withgott and Brennan, *Essential Environment: The Science Behind the Stories*, 3rd. ed., p.371.

_____ 3. Which sentence is the topic sentence of the paragraph?
      a.   sentence 1   b.   sentence 2
      c.   sentence 3   d.   sentence 5

4 [1]Cyberspace has become a fertile field for illegal activity. [2]With the uses of new technology and equipment which cannot be policed by traditional methods, cyberstalkng has replaced traditional methods of stalking and harassment. [3]In addition, cyberstalking has led to offline incidents of violent crime. [4]Clearly, police and prosecutors need to be aware of the escalating number of cyberstalking events and devise strategies to resolve these problems through the criminal justice system.

—Adapted from Schmalleger, *Criminal Justice: A Brief Introduction*, 8th ed., p. 53.

_____ 4. Which sentence is the topic sentence of the paragraph?

    a. sentence 1   b. sentence 2

    c. sentence 3   d. sentence 4

5 [1]In order to meet customer needs, companies have to efficiently manage many concerns, including their image and reputation. [2]If a scandal (such as a tampered-with consumer product) breaks out, how does the company handle it? [3]Does it act like nothing happened, or does it quickly try to remedy the problem? [4]Often companies handle image problems by sending out positive news to counteract bad news. [5]For example, when one drug fails in a pharmaceutical company, management puts out news about a promising drug that is undergoing research and development. [6]In a movie production company, a failed movie is pushed aside, and the promotion effort switches to the next upcoming film.

—Adapted from Goldsmith, *Consumer Economics: Issues and Behaviors*, 2nd ed., pp.172–173.

_____ 5. Which sentence is the topic sentence of the paragraph?

    a. sentence 2   b. sentence 3

    c. sentence 4   d. sentence 5

6 [1]The central nervous system is vital to proper functioning of the entire body, so it is no surprise that it is well protected against physical injury and disease. [2]First, the CNS is protected by bone. [3]The brain is encased in the skull, and the spinal cord is enclosed in a hollow channel within the vertebrae. [4]This shell of bone around the central nervous system helps shield it form physical trauma. [5]Second, the CNS is enclosed by three membranes of connective tissue, called meninges. [6]These three meninges protect the neurons of the CNS and the blood vessels that service them. [7]Third, the CNS is bathed in its own special liquid, called cerebrospinal fluid, which fills the spaces. [8]In addition to serving as a liquid shock absorber around the brain and spinal cord, cerebrospinal fluid tends to isolate the central nervous system from infections.

—Adapted from Johnson, *Human Biology: Concepts and Current Issues*, 5th ed., pp. 256–257.

_____ 6. Which sentence is the topic sentence of the paragraph?

    a. sentence 1   b. sentence 2

    c. sentence 4   d. sentence 6

7 [1]More than a quarter century ago, to curb its skyrocketing population, the Chinese government passed regulations limiting families to one child each. [2]As a result, Chinese children—known as 'little emperors and empresses'—have been showered with attention and luxuries under what's known as the "six-pocket syndrome." [3]As many as six adults—two parents and four doting grandparents—may be indulging the whims of each only child. [4]Parents with only one child at home now spend about 40 percent of their income on their cherished child.

—Adapted from Kotler and Armstrong, *Principles of Marketing*, 13th ed., p. 70.

_____ 7. Which sentence is the topic sentence of the paragraph?
    a. sentence 1   b. sentence 2
    c. sentence 4   d. sentence 6

8 [1]Some people with strong faith may be disturbed by the thought of sociologists turning a scientific eye on what they hold sacred. [2]However, a sociology study of religion is no threat to anyone's faith. [3]Sociologists study religion just as they study the family. [4]Sociologists want to understand religious experience around the world. [5]They want to understand how religion is tied to other social institutions. [6]They make no judgments that a specific religion is right or wrong in terms of ultimate truth.

—Adapted from Macionis, *Sociology*, 13th ed., p. 489.

_____ 8. Which sentence is the topic sentence of the paragraph?
    a. sentence 1   b. sentence 2
    c. sentence 4   d. sentence 6

9 [1]Many graduating students are facing years of paying on college loans. [2]Seeing years of financial obligation, they often ask the question, "How can I start over when my past keeps reaching into the future and pulling me into the present?" [3]The fact is, though, that the rewards of developing a financial plan and budget are worth small sacrifices in order to give you control over spending and saving. [4]Planning and budgeting don't come naturally. [5]Showing financial restraint isn't as much fun a spending with reckless abandon, but it's a lot more fun than winding up broke and homeless. [6]Making and sticking with a plan isn't necessarily easy, and it often involves what some people would consider sacrifices, such as getting a job over spring break instead of going down to Panama City to be on MTV's Spring Break, or just skipping that daily designer coffee.

—Adapted from Keown, Personal Finance: Turning Money into Wealth, 5th ed., p. 30.

_____ 9. Which sentence is the topic sentence of the paragraph?
    a. sentence 1   b. sentence 2
    c. sentence 3   d. sentence 4

10 [1]Women seem to be more engaged in listening than do men for several reasons. [2]First, men and women feed back to the speaker different types of listening cues and consequently show that they're listening in different ways. [3]In conversation, a woman is more apt to give lots of listening cues—interjecting "Yeah" or "Uh-huh," nodding in agreement and smiling. [4]On the other hand, a man is more likely to listen quietly, without giving lots of listening cues as feedback. [5]Second, women make more eye contact when listening than do men, who are more apt to look around and often away from the speaker.

—Adapted from DeVito, *The Interpersonal Communication Book*, 12th ed., p. 88.

_____ 10. Which sentence is the topic sentence of the paragraph?
    a. sentence 1   b. sentence 2
    c. sentence 3   d. sentence 4

Chapter 5: Locating Stated Main Ideas
LAB 5.2 PRACTICE EXERCISE 2

Name _____ Section _____ Date _____ Score (number correct) _____ x 10 = _____

Objective: To identify the main idea in a paragraph by considering the supporting details.

Directions: Identify the topic sentence of each paragraph.

1 [1]Market researchers carefully examine the shopping habits of consumers and have found three characteristics that attract customers. [2]One thing people want in a fast-food chain is the kind of variety that Wendy's and Taco Bell provide. [3]Another trait that lures shoppers is convenience. [4]That is why you often find Wal-Mart at a location near an interstate exit. [5]A third characteristic that is popular with consumers is reasonable prices. [6]Target offers merchandise at affordable prices. [7]In fact, Wendy's, Taco Bell, Wal-Mart, and Target are all examples of successful chains that offer consumers variety and convenience at reasonable prices.

_____ 1. Which sentence is the topic sentence of the paragraph?
   a. sentence 1   c. sentence 5
   b. sentence 2   d. sentence 7

2 [1]Sexually transmitted diseases (STDs) are infections that are passed from one person to another by sexual contact. [2]STDs are caused by germs such as bacteria, fungi, and viruses. [3]Antibiotics, like penicillin, often cure STDs caused by bacteria and fungi. [4]For example, syphilis and gonorrhea are both curable if treated in time with antibiotics. [5]However, many STDs caused by viruses cannot be cured. [6]For example, there is currently no cure for genital herpes.

_____ 2. Which sentence is the topic sentence of the paragraph?
   a. sentence 1   c. sentence 5
   b. sentence 2   d. sentence 6

3 [1]Today, some people may think of wrestling as more of a staged circus act than a real sport. [2]However, this has not always been the case. [3]Wrestling has a long and proud history. [4]Early man may have wrestled with animals for survival. [5]Because it requires strength and flexibility, wrestling became part of the first Olympic Games held in Greece 3,000 years ago. [6]Wrestling has attracted people of courage and leadership. [7]For example, George Washington, the first president of the United States, was a leading wrestler in the Virginia colony.

_____ 3. Which sentence is the topic sentence of the paragraph?
   a. sentence 1   c. sentence 3
   b. sentence 2   d. sentence 7

4 [1]Few of us could swim in the ocean comfortably after seeing filmmaker Steven Spielberg's terrifying movie *Jaws*. [2]In his hit movie, *E. T. the Extra- Terrestrial,* Spielberg created a sweet, funny film about a being from outer space. [3]In 1985, he gave us *The Color Purple,* a moving picture about a black family in the South that earned him a Best Director nomination. [4]Steven Spielberg has created some of the most successful and popular films of the 1970s and 1980s.

_____ 4. Which sentence is the topic sentence of the paragraph?
      a. sentence 1   c. sentence 3
      b. sentence 2   d. sentence 4

5 [1]Although many women have worked for equality, few have become well known for their success. [2]Four women, however, are widely recognized for their work in the cause of equal treatment for everyone. [3]Lucretia Mott (1793–1880) started a women's antislavery society. [4]She also organized the first women's rights convention. [5]Sojourner Truth (1797–1883) bravely spoke out for freedom and independence for both blacks and women. [6]Finally, Elizabeth Cady Stanton (1815–1902) and Lucy Stone (1818–1893) began the fight for women's right to vote. [7]Each of these women worked hard for the rights of others.

_____ 5. Which sentence is the topic sentence of the paragraph?
      a. sentence 1   c. sentence 5
      b. sentence 2   d. sentence 7

6 [1]The endangered leatherback sea turtle is finally thriving in Florida. [2]Early in the 2001 nesting season, leatherback sea turtles laid eggs in the largest number of nests in decades. [3]By June of that year, these turtles, which can end up weighing 700 pounds, had filled 18 nests along the coast of Volusia County, Canaveral National Seashore, and Flagler County. [4]At last, 30 years after the Endangered Species Act was passed, these turtles have made a comeback.

_____ 6. Which sentence is the topic sentence of the paragraph?
      a. sentence 1   c. sentence 3
      b. sentence 2   d. sentence 4

7 [1]On a typical summer day, dark clouds quietly rise and gather unnoticed until they block out the sun in the afternoon sky. [2]A wind begins to blow until it surges to 35 miles per hour. [3]Lightning sparks a fire by striking a group of trees. [4]Another bolt of lightning pierces the roof of a house, leaving a smoldering hole in both the roof and the kitchen ceiling. [5]A summer thunderstorm can pose serious danger.

_____ 7. Which sentence is the topic sentence of the paragraph?
      a. Sentence 1   c. Sentence 3
      b. Sentence 2   d. Sentence 5

Food Myths

[1]The number of myths about physical fitness and nutrition or diet grows every year. [2]One myth concerns which foods are best to increase the body's ability to perform. [3]The public often thinks of winning athletes as experts and looks to them for advice. [4]Some star athletes may therefore try to convince people that a certain food or drink is at the root of their success. [5]The truth is, there are no miracle foods to improve physical fitness. [6]People who exercise on a regular basis have specific nutritional needs and must adjust their diet.

[7]A common example of a myth about food deals with strength training. [8]Some people believe that extra amounts of protein are needed for muscle growth. [9]In fact, many bodybuilders take in large amounts of protein to add to their normal diet. [10]However, research has shown that the protein needed by most bodybuilders is met by a normal, well-balanced diet. [11]Therefore, body-builders should meet their protein needs by healthy eating from the food pyramid, not from simply adding protein to their diets.

_____ 8. Which sentence is the topic sentence of the first paragraph?
   a. sentence 1   c. sentence 5
   b. sentence 2   d. sentence 6

_____ 9. Which sentence is the topic sentence of the second paragraph?
   a. sentence 7   c. sentence 9
   b. sentence 8   d. sentence 11

_____ 10. Which sentence states the central idea of the passage?
   a. Extra protein is not needed for strength training.
   b. Winning athletes sometime give false information about how they achieved success.
   c. Physical fitness is best achieved by healthy eating and regular exercise, not by succumbing to food myths.
   d. A normal, well-balanced diet contains enough protein for the body.

Chapter 5: Locating Stated Main Ideas
LAB 5.3 REVIEW TEST 1

Name _____ Section _____ Date _____ Score (number correct) _____ x 10 = _____

Directions: Identify the topic sentence of each paragraph.

1 [1]You may well have already taken part in transactions involving financial incentives as policy tools. [2]For example, many cities charge residents for waste disposal according to the amount of waste they generate. [3]Clearly, at all levels, from the local to the international, financial incentives can reduce environmental impact while minimizing overall costs to industry and easing concerns about the intrusiveness of government regulation. [4]Other examples include cities that place taxes or disposal fees on items that require costly safe disposal, such as tires and motor oil. [5]Still others give rebates to residents who buy water-efficient toilets and appliances, because the rebates can cost the city less than upgrading its sewage treatment system. [6]Likewise, power companies sometimes offer discounts to customers who buy high-efficiency light bulbs and appliances, because doing so is cheaper for the utilities than expanding the generating capacity of their plants.

—Adapted from Withgott and Brennan, *Environment: The Science behind the Stories,*
3rd ed., pp. 82–83

_____ 1. Which sentence is the topic sentence of the paragraph?
   a. sentence 1   c. sentence 3
   b. sentence 2   d. sentence 6

2 [1]The rate of teen births in the United States has gone down steadily. [2]In 1996, 500,000 babies were born to mothers who were 15 to 19 years of age. [3]About 75 percent of these young women were not married. [4]An additional 11,000 babies were born to mothers who were 14 or younger. [5]All of these mothers were unmarried. [6]Despite the decline in the teen birthrate, the number of teen births to unmarried young women continues to grow. [7]One reason for the teen birthrate is poverty. [8]A second reason is low academic success. [9]A third, and major, reason is sexual coercion. [10]As many as 50 to 70 percent of babies born to girls aged 11 to 18 are fathered by men who are four to seven years older than the mothers. [11]The reasons and numbers of teen births are still alarming.

—Adapted from Renzetti and Curran, *Women, Men, and Society,* 4th ed., pp. 156–57.

_____ 2. Which sentence is the topic sentence of the paragraph?
   a. sentence 1   c. sentence 5
   b. sentence 2   d. sentence 11

3 [1]Even before a person begins to walk and talk, she becomes aware of the rules that govern her behavior. [2]Mother says, "No!" whenever she touches the television. [3]She learns that food should not be thrown on the floor or eaten with fingers. [4]As the person internalizes these rules and values, a Parent ego state develops. [5]The Parent ego applies self-control to a person's behavior. [6]There are two forms of parent behavior. [7]One is the Nurturing Parent, and the other is the Critical Parent. [8]The Nurturing Parent is supportive and helpful. [9]Children copy this behavior in their play as they pretend to be doctors, nurses, and other caregivers. [10]The Critical Parent sets up rules about what is "good" and "bad."

—Adapted from Brownell, *Listening: Attitudes, Principles, and Skills,* 2nd ed., pp. 274–75.

62

_____ 3. Which sentence is the topic sentence of the paragraph?
      a.   sentence 1   c.   sentence 9
      b.   sentence 6   d.   sentence 10

4 ¹Matt Drudge used the Internet in the early 1990s to post a story just on a hunch. ²Drudge was 30 years old when he broke his first story about Monica Lewinsky's relationship with President Clinton. ³This relationship became the biggest political scandal of the 1990s. ⁴Drudge had never been trained in journalism or hired by any media outlet. ⁵He had not verified the story, nor did he do any research. ⁶All he had to go on was a rumor that *Newsweek* had been working on the story. ⁷*Newsweek* had decided not to print the story in that week's issue. ⁸But for Drudge, a rumor was good enough to report. ⁹No editor was going to tell him that he needed confirmation, because Drudge worked on his own. ¹⁰He didn't have to worry about the damage to his publication because he didn't have one. ¹¹He got his "Drudge Report" out through an email list and by posting it on his Web site (www.drudgereport.com). ¹²When Drudge hit the Enter button on his computer to post the story, he knew his life would be changed forever, and for some time so would the nation's. ¹³Matt Drudge and his brand of cyber-reporting have changed the whole news cycle in America.

      —Adapted from Edwards, Wattenberg, and Lineberry, *Government in America: People, Politics, and Policy,* 5th ed., Brief Version, p. 170.

_____ 4. Which sentence is the topic sentence of the paragraph?
      a.   sentence 1   c.   sentence 7
      b.   sentence 3   d.   sentence 13

5 ¹Japanese diets are very healthy. ²They are low in high-cholesterol items such as red meat and dairy products, and they are high in mineral-rich foods such as seafood and seaweed. ³Many kinds of fish are eaten, such as salmon, cod, flounder, tuna, and many others. ⁴Vegetables are equally abundant and come in an endless variety. ⁵A few of these vegetables include leeks, white radishes, ginger, eggplant, bamboo sprouts, and wasabi (which is similar to horseradish). ⁶Noodles and tofu are also very popular. ⁷Of course, one common staple of all Japanese diets is rice. ⁸1t is eaten for breakfast, lunch, and dinner. ⁹As proof of their good health, Japanese have a longer lifespan than most other nations and a startlingly low rate of heart disease.

      —Adapted from Nakamura, *Health in America: A Multicultural Perspective,* Copyright © 1999, p. 127.

_____ 5. Which sentence is the topic sentence of the paragraph?
      a.   sentence 1   c.   sentence 7
      b.   sentence 3   d.   sentence 9

Three Waves of Immigration

[1]The United States has often been called a melting pot, which refers to a mixture of cultures, ideas, and peoples. [2]This mixture of people occurred because of three waves of immigration. [3]The first wave of people came before the Civil War. [4]This group was made up of English, Irish, German, and Scandinavian people. [5]After the Civil War, Italians, Jews, Poles, and Russians made up the second wave of people. [6]This group was largest during the first decade of the twentieth century. [7]Almost all these people passed through Ellis Island in New York. [8]Recently, a third wave of immigrants are Hispanics from Cuba, Central America, and Mexico. [9]Along with these diverse groups, people have come here from Vietnam, Korea, China, and Japan. [10]Each group of people brings with them their dreams, their beliefs, and their special ways of life.

—Adapted from Edwards, Wattenberg, and Lineberry, *Government in America: People, Politics, and Policy,* 5th ed., Brief Version, p. 138.

_____ 6. Which sentence is the topic sentence of the paragraph?
     a. sentence 2   c. sentence 7
     b. sentence 4   d. sentence 10

7 [1]Journalists cannot always make sure that their stories are true. [2]Yet they can make an extra effort to be truthful and to avoid lying. [3]In July 1996, *Newsweek* writer Joe Klein admitted that he had written the best-selling novel *Primary Colors.* [4]The book sold 1.2 million copies with the name "Anonymous" on its cover and title page. [5]Admitting he had written the book may seem minor. [6]However, he had denied several times that he had written the book. [7]The book was a harsh view of President Clinton's 1992 primary campaign. [8]Journalists around the country attacked Klein for lying. [9]He replied that he had a right to privacy in writing the novel. [10]He then asked whether his denials had hurt anyone. [11]Critics noted that making around $6 million from a book and movie rights is his right. [12]However, readers might not trust journalism, knowing that powerful journalists are willing to lie to make money.

—Adapted from Folkerts and Lacy, *The Media in Your Life: An Introduction to Mass Communication*, 2nd ed., p. 361.

_____ 7. Which sentence is the topic sentence of the paragraph?
     a. sentence 1   c. sentence 8
     b. sentence 5   d. sentence 12

[1]The total number of insect species is greater than the total of all other species put together. **Entomology** is a branch of biology that specializes in the study of insects. [3]Insects live in almost every terrestrial habitat and in fresh water, and flying insects fill the air. [4]Insects are rare in the seas, where crustaceans are the dominant arthopods.

[5]Insects have a number of common features. Like the grasshopper in Figure 18.12A, most have a three-part body, consisting of a head, a thorax, and an abdomen. [6]The head usually bears a pair of sensory antennae and a pair of eyes. [7]Several pairs of mouthparts are adapted for particular kinds of eating—for example, for chewing plant material in grasshoppers; for lapping up fluids in houseflies; and for piercing skin and sucking blood in mosquitoes. [8]Most adult insects have three pairs of legs and one or two pairs of wings.(…)

A. Order Orthoptera. [9]The grasshopper represents this group, which contains about 13,000 species. [10]Other orthopterans are the crickets, katydids, locusts. [11]These insects have biting and chewing mouthparts, and most species are herbivorous. [12]They have large hind legs adapted for jumping and two pairs of wings (one leathery, one membranous). [13]Males commonly make courtship sounds by rubbing together body parts, such as a ridge on the hind leg.

—Adapted from Campbell, Reece, Taylor, and Simon, *Biology: Concepts and Connections*, 5th ed., p. 382.

_____ 8. Which sentence is the topic sentence of the second paragraph?
   a. sentence 5   c. sentence 7
   b. sentence 6   d. sentence 8

_____ 9. Which sentence is the topic sentence of the third paragraph?
   a. sentence 9   c. sentence 11
   b. sentence 10   d. sentence 12

_____ 10. Which sentence is the central idea of the passage?
   a. The total number of insect species is greater than the total of all other species combined.
   b. **Entomology** is a branch of biology that specializes in the study of insects.
   c. Insects have a number of common features.
   d. The grasshopper represents this group, which contains about 13,000 species.

Chapter 5: Locating Stated Main Ideas
LAB 5.4 REVIEW TEST 2

Name _____ Section _____ Date _____ Score (number correct) _____ x 10 = _____

Directions: Identify the topic sentence of each paragraph.

1 [1]Because US. Society is racially, ethnically, and religiously diverse, all of us have to work with people who differ from ourselves. [2]The same is true of sociologists. [3]Learning, in advance, the ways of life of any category of people can ease the work of a sociologist and ensure that there will be no hard feelings when the work is finished. [4]For example, a person's request to speak privately with a Hispanic woman may provoke suspicion or outright disapproval from her husband or father.

—Adapted from Macionis, *Sociology*, 13th ed., p. 39

_____ 1. Which sentence is the topic sentence of the paragraph?
        a. sentence 1   b. sentence 2
        c. sentence 3   d. sentence 4

2 [1]Not all crimes have clearly identifiable victims. [2]Some, such as murder, do not have victims who survive. [3]Where there is an identifiable surviving victim, however, he or she is often one of the most forgotten people in the courtroom. [4]Although the victim may have been profoundly affected by the crime itself, he or she may not even be permitted to participate directly in the trial process. [5]It is not unusual for crime victims to be totally unaware of the final outcome of a case that intimately concerns them.

—Adapted from Schmalleger, *Criminal Justice: A Brief Introduction*, 8th ed., p. 288.

_____ 2. Which sentence is the topic sentence of the paragraph?
        a. sentence 1   b. sentence 2
        c. sentence 3   d. sentence 4

3 [1]Like words and gestures, silence serves several important communication functions. [2]Silence allows the speaker time to think, time to formulate and organize his or her verbal communications. [3]In addition, sometimes people use silence as a weapon to hurt others. [4]We often speak of giving someone "the silent treatment." [5]After a conflict, for example one or both individuals may remain silent as a kind of punishment. [6]Finally, sometimes silence is used as a response to personal anxiety, shyness, or threats. [7]You may feel anxious or shy among new people and prefer to remain silent.

—Adapted from DeVito, *The Interpersonal Communication Book*, 12th ed., p.141.

_____ 3. Which sentence is the topic sentence of the paragraph?
        a. sentence 1   b. sentence 2
        c. sentence 3   d. sentence 4

4   [1]From ancient times, cities have drawn in resources from outlying rural areas through trade, persuasion, or conquest. [2]Today, however cheap transportation and powerful technologies enabled by fossil fuels have allowed some cities to thrive even in resource-poor regions. [3]The Dallas-Fort Worth area benefits from—and depends on—oil-fueled transportation by interstate highways and a major airport. [4]Southwestern cities such as Los Angeles, Las Vegas, and Phoenix are located in desert regions, requiring them to appropriate water from distant sources to support their populations.

—Adapted from Withgott and Brennan, *Essential Environment: The Science Behind the Stories*, 3rd ed., pp. 187–188.

_____ 4. Which sentence is the topic sentence of the paragraph?
   a.   sentence 1   b.   sentence 2
   c.   sentence 3   d.   sentence 4

5   [1]Autistic people may not like to touch or be touched, do not communicate well if at all, and tend not to make eye contact. [2]In one study, autistic children and non-autistic children were asked to imitate the facial expressions while researchers measured their neural activity in the mirror neuron system in the brain. [3]Although both groups of children were able to imitate the expressions, the autistic children showed no neural activity in the mirror system while doing so. [4]The non-autistic children did show such mirror system activity. [5]This study suggests that autism may be due at least in part to a faulty mirror system in the brain.

—Adapted from Ciccarelli and White, *Psychology*, 2nd ed., p. 83.

_____ 5. Which sentence is the topic sentence of the paragraph?
   a.   sentence 1   b.   sentence 2
   c.   sentence 3   d.   sentence 5

6   [1]So much has happened in the past few years. [2]We've had toys recalled because of lead in the paint, outbreaks of E. coli from contaminated spinach, a salmonella outbreak from peanut butter, and pets dying from imported wheat gluten tainted with melamine. [3]If ever there was a time when consumers and their safety were in the forefront, this is it. [4]On top of all this, national and world economies are going through ups and downs and populations continue to grow. [5]The U.S. population is over 300 million, and the world population has swelled to over 6.6 billion.

—Adapted from Goldsmith, *Consumer Economics: Issues and Behaviors*, 2nd ed., p. xv.

_____ 6. Which sentence is the topic sentence of the paragraph?
   a.   sentence 1   b.   sentence 2
   c.   sentence 3   d.   sentence 4

7 [1]To increase mindfulness in general, try these suggestions. [2]Create and recreate categories. [3]Learn to see objects, events, and people as belonging to a wide variety of categories. [4]Try to see, for example your prospective romantic partner in a variety of roles—child, parent, employer, neighbor, friend, financial contributor, and so on. [5]Next, be open to new information and points of view, even when these contradict your most firmly held stereotypes. [6]New information forces you to reconsider what might be outmoded ways of thinking. [7]New information can help you challenge long-held but now inappropriate beliefs and attitudes. [8]Finally, beware of relying too heavily on first impressions. [9]Treat your first impressions as hypotheses that need further investigation. [10]Be prepared to revise reject, or accept these initial impressions.

_____ 7. Which sentence is the topic sentence of the paragraph?
     a.   sentence 1   b.   sentence 3
     c.   sentence 5   d.   sentence 10

[1]Presently, over 50 percent of Americans receive some government health care entitlements, such as Medicare or Medicaid, and most Americans have medical insurance. [2]As a result, there simply isn't any incentive for patients, doctors, or hospitals to exercise restraint in medical billing. [3]If you aren't paying out of your own pocket, why should you care what your bills are? [4]And if these bills are certain to be paid, why should doctors or hospitals care how much they charge?

[6]Other reasons health care is so costly concern the high expense of new medical treatments and the cost of litigation. Today's medical care has become extremely sophisticated. [7]For example, it now takes 12 years and costs over $230 million to develop, test, and certify a new drug, and drug companies are passing these costs on to patients. [8]Finally, the cost of litigation from malpractice suits has skyrocketed. [9]It's not uncommon for doctors to pay malpractice insurance premiums of $150,000 or $250,000 per year. [10]These costs, too, are then passed directly on to patients.

—Adapted from Keown, *Personal Finance: Turning Money into Wealth*, 5th ed., p. 276.

_____ 8. Which sentence is the topic sentence of the first paragraph?
     a.   sentence 1   b.   sentence 2
     c.   sentence 3   d.   sentence 4

_____ 9. Which sentence is the topic sentence of the second paragraph?
     a.   sentence 6   b.   sentence 7
     c.   sentence 8   d.   sentence 9

_____ 10. Which sentence is the central idea of the passage?
     a.   New medical treatments are driving up the cost of health care.
     b.   The costs of expensive malpractice insurance and expensive litigation trials are simply passed along to the patients.
     c.   The development of new drugs has become far too expensive and is having an adverse effect on medical care.
     d.   Expensive litigation, costly new medical treatments, and lack of incentive to lower billing costs are all reasons for today's high health care costs.

Name _____ Section _____ Date _____ Score (number correct) _____ x 10 = _____

Directions: Identify the topic sentence of each paragraph.

[1]The USS *Monitor* was a Civil War ironclad, which, along with the USS *Merrimac,* changed the course of U.S. naval history. [2]For 140 years, the *Monitor* has remained at the bottom of the Graveyard of the Atlantic, a stretch off the coast of Cape Hatteras, North Carolina, after meeting its demise in a treacherous storm. [3]An archaeology team has excavated the gun turret of the *Monitor,* however, and historians are excited about several discoveries. [4]First, the remains of several bodies were discovered in that low, tower-like structure. [5]Another discovery was a gold ring with an inscription, which historians hope will aid them in identifying at least one of the bodies.

_____ 1.   Which sentence is the topic sentence of the paragraph?
    a.   sentence 1   c.   sentence 3
    b.   sentence 2   d.   sentence 5

[1]Currently, a 1943 penny is worth a lot more than one cent. [2]Because of the need for copper during World War II, the U.S. Mint made only a limited number of copper pennies. [3]Most pennies were made of steel that year because the government needed the copper for wiring, critical to wartime manufacturing. [4]Some people speculate that the copper pennies were actually made by mistake. [5]Consequently, a 1943 copper penny is now worth a small fortune. [6]For example, in 1996, a 1943 copper penny sold for $82,500. [7]Likewise, because nickel was so important for making armor plating, the U.S. Mint actually made nickels out of silver, which was less valuable at the time than it is now. [8]Therefore, some currency made during World War II is now actually worth a great deal more than its face value

_____ 2.   Which sentence is the topic sentence of the paragraph?
    a.   sentence 1   c.   sentence 5
    b.   sentence 2   d.   sentence 8

[1]The word *perseverance* means continuing despite the odds. [2]Derek Redmond exemplified perseverance in the 1992 Olympics in Barcelona, Spain. [3]Although he was expected to win the gold medal in the 400-meter race, he met with disaster after a great start when he pulled his hamstring, and the pain brought him down onto the track. [4]Although the race ended in a short time and medics begged him to lie down on a stretcher, Redmond continued his painful hobble to the finish line. [5]Suddenly, a man broke away from the security guards, put his arm around Redmond, and told him they would finish together. [6]The man was Redmond's father, and together they completed the race, to the cheering of thousands of fans.

_____ 3.   Which sentence is the topic sentence of the paragraph?
    a.   sentence 1   c.   sentence 5
    b.   sentence 2   d.   sentence 6

[1]Have you ever wondered how writers choose the names of their characters? [2]For example, in Stephen King's novel *The Green Mile,* we meet John Coffey, the protagonist, who is unjustly accused of a crime and later executed, despite the miracles he performs. [3]His initials "J.C." would prompt a reader to predict that the character's death may lead to some good for those around him, despite the injustice of the ending. [4]Another example is Jack Cardinal in David Baldacci's *Wish You Well.* [5]Again, we see the initials "J.C.," but we also realize that it is no coincidence that Cardinal, the family's last name, is also the state bird of Virginia, the setting of the novel. [6]Writers frequently use characters' names to indicate their personal attributes and the role they play in the work.

_____ 4. Which sentence is the topic sentence of the paragraph?
     a. sentence 1   c   sentence 5
     b. sentence 3   d. sentence 6

[1]You are working in the kitchen and suddenly cut yourself on one of your sharpest knives. [2]Although you immediately apply pressure, the bleeding continues. [3]What should you do? [4]Try sprinkling some black pepper or ground sage on the cut. [5]Are you looking for a natural stress reliever? [6]Then light a lavender-scented candle. [7]Finally, if you want a quick bit of mental stimulation, sniff some peppermint. [8]Many home remedies such as these are promoted by herbalists—people who use herbs and other natural ingredients—rather than commercial drugs.

_____ 5. Which sentence is the topic sentence of the paragraph?
     a. sentence 1   c. sentence 7
     b. sentence 3   d. sentence 8

[1]In a cooperative group, the crucial elements of trust are openness and sharing on the one hand and acceptance, support, and cooperative intentions on the other. [2]Working cooperatively with others requires openness and sharing, which in turn are determined by the expression of acceptance, support, and cooperative intentions in the group. [3]Openness is the sharing of information, ideas, thoughts, feelings, and reactions to the issue the group is pursuing. [4]Sharing is the offering of your materials and resources to others in order to help them move the group toward goal accomplishment. [5]Acceptance is the communication of high regard toward others and their contributions to the group's work. [6]Support is the communication to others that you recognize their strengths and believe in their capability to manage productively the situation they are in. [7]Cooperative intentions are the expectations that you are going to behave cooperatively and that every group member will also cooperate in achieving the group's goal.

—Johnson and Johnson, *Joining Together: Group Theory and Group Skills*, 7th ed., p. 134.

_____ 6. Which sentence is the topic sentence of the paragraph?
     a. sentence 1   c. sentence 6
     b. sentence 4   d. sentence 7

[1]Acceptance is probably the first and deepest concern to arise in a group. [2]Acceptance of others usually begins with acceptance of oneself. [3]Group members need to accept themselves before they can fully accept others. [4]Acceptance is the key to reducing anxiety and fears about being vulnerable. [5]Defensive feelings of fear and distrust are common blocks to the functioning of a person and to the development of constructive relationships. [6]Certainly, if a person does not feel accepted, the frequency and depth of participation in the group will decrease. [7]To build trust and to deepen relationships among group members, each member needs to be able to communicate acceptance, support, and cooperativeness.

—Johnson and Johnson, *Joining Together: Group Theory and Group Skills*, 7th ed., p. 134.

_____ 7. Which sentence is the topic sentence of the paragraph?
a. sentence 1   c. sentence 5
b. sentence 3   d. sentence 7

Changing Relationships

[1]In general, as people age, they interact with fewer people, but these contacts tend to be close and strong. [2]Relationships earlier in life tend to include more friends than relatives, but with age the mix reverses. [3]More time is spent with relatives than with friends. [4]In later life, a relationship long inactive can be picked up and brought back with minimal effort. [5]After young adulthood, attitudes and behaviors become stable. [6]This stability makes it easy to "know" someone again even after a long lapse.

[7]During young adulthood, people care that their relationships with friends and relatives are equitable— that no one gives more than he or she receives. [8]As people grow older, such concerns fade into the background. [9]In successful marriages, couples think of themselves as a team. [10]They do not see themselves as separate people who are in constant debate. [11]Because they are in it for the long haul, people trust that the balance of favors and repayment will even out over time. [12]Adults become more stable and giving as they grow older.

—Adapted from Kosslyn and Rosenberg, *Psychology: The Brain, the Person, the World*, Copyright © 2001, p. 425.

_____ 8. Which sentence is the topic sentence of the first paragraph?
a. sentence 1   c. sentence 4
b. sentence 3   d. sentence 6

_____ 9. Which sentence is the topic sentence of the second paragraph?
a. sentence 7   c. sentence 11
b. sentence 9   d. sentence 12

_____ 10. Which sentence is the central idea of the passage?
a. Relationships change as people age.
b. Relationships earlier in life tend to include more friends than relatives.
c. People begin to trust that the balance of favors and repayment will even out over time.
d. Attitudes and behaviors become more stable after adulthood.

Name _____ Section _____ Date _____ Score (number correct) _____ x 10 = _____

Directions: Identify the topic sentence of each paragraph.

[1]Commercials remain the soul of network television. [2]Those who count such things tell us that the average American sees at least 32,000 of them in a given year. [3]In a sense, they represent a minor art form in that they have to make their point in 30 seconds; unless they are successful, a multibillion-dollar industry could disappear from the earth. [4]In addition, both manufacturers and producers know they are up against the mightiest challenge ever faced by the industry: remote control. [5]You can change channels in an instant during the commercial break. [6]You can summon up the little screen that allows you to watch two channels at once. [7]At the very least, you can press the "mute" button so you don't have to listen.

_____ 1. Which sentence is the topic sentence of the paragraph?
     a. sentence 1   c. sentence 5
     b. sentence 3   d. sentence 7

[1]If personal letters are time-consuming and close relationships are on the wane, written communication to oneself is relatively easy. [2]Stationery departments still carry a large assortment of diaries. [3]Gwendolyn, the heroine of Oscar Wilde's *The Importance of Being Earnest,* insists she never goes anywhere without her diary, especially when she takes the train, because "one should always have something sensational to read ...." [4]The implication is that a diary for her becomes a place to keep her wildest imaginings, her private fantasies. [5]Admittedly, this is one way of getting a perspective on yourself. [6]At least you know what your life is *not.* [7]The more conservative of us simply write a summary of the day's events, a harmless, if not especially valuable, exercise, unless we are willing to probe behind the events. [8]By far the recommended means of examining our lives carefully is the personal journal.

—Janaro and Altschuler, *The Art of Being Human* 6th ed., p. 81.

_____ 2. Which sentence is the topic sentence of the paragraph?
     a. sentence 1   c. sentence 5
     b. sentence 2   d. sentence 8

[1]During the peak of the presidential scandals, the Internet browser often receives the most sensational rumors several times a day, sometimes attributed to a source, sometimes not. [2]Most often the news service of the Internet consists merely of news flashes coming into centralized communications sources such as the Associated Press. [3]While entire news and magazine articles *are* available, the Internet encourages browsing (as opposed to serious reading) by providing a summary that can be read in a minute or two. [4]As you scroll down the screen, quick read follows quick read, and there's neither time nor space for full reporting. [5]Consequently, Internet news is usually very short and to the point.

—Adapted from Janaro and Altshuler, *The Art of Being Human*, 6th ed., p. 90.

_____ 3. Which sentence is the topic sentence of the paragraph?
      a.   sentence 1   c.   sentence 4
      b.   sentence 2   d.   sentence 5

[1]Many early myths were designed to explain nature, and many early rituals were efforts to control it. [2]In Scandinavian communities, for example, the fertility deity was Freyr, who was thought to bring rich harvests to the earth. [3]He did so by wooing a maiden, symbolizing the union of earth and sky. [4]Rituals that honored Freyr and the abundance he gave were essential for survival. [5]In almost all early cultures, help from the gods was needed if crops should fail or were insufficient, for then the mortals had to turn to the sea, where food could be found only if the storm god were placated.

—Janaro and Altshuler, *The Art of Being Human,* 6th ed., p. 513.

_____ 4. Which sentence is the topic sentence of the paragraph?
      a.   sentence 1   c.   sentence 4
      b.   sentence 2   d.   sentence 5

[1]Although trust exists in relationships, not in people, there has been some attempt to measure individual differences in willingness to trust others. [2]Rotter (1971) developed the **Interpersonal Trust Scale** to distinguish between people who have a tendency to trust others and those who tend to distrust. [3]A high truster tends to say, "I will trust a person until I have clear evidence that he or she cannot be trusted." [4]A low truster tends to say, "I will not trust a person until there is clear evidence that her or she can be trusted." [5]High trusters tend to be more trustworthy than low trusters. [6]High trusters, compared with low trusters, are (a) more likely to give others a second chance, respect the rights of others, and be liked and sought out as friends (by both low- and high-trust people), and (b) less likely to lie and be unhappy, conflicted, or maladjusted.

—Johnson and Johnson, *Joining Together: Group Theory and Group Skills*, 7th ed., p. 138.

_____ 5. Which sentence is the topic sentence of the paragraph?
      a.   sentence 1   c.   sentence 6
      b.   sentence 2   d.   sentence 7

[1]Communication is the basis for all human interaction and for all group functioning. [2]Every group must take in and use information. [3]The very existence of a group depends on communication, on exchanging information and transmitting meaning. [4]All cooperative action is contingent upon effective communication, and our daily lives are filled with one communication experience after another. [5]Through communication, members of groups reach some understanding of one another, build trust, coordinate their actions, plan strategies for goal accomplishment, agree upon a division of labor, conduct all group activities, and even exchange insults. [6]Thus, it is through communication that the members interact, and effective communication is a prerequisite for every aspect of group functioning.

—Adapted from Johnson and Johnson, *Joining Together: Group Theory and Group Skills,*
7th ed., p. 142.

_____ 6. Which sentence is the topic sentence of the paragraph?
      a.   sentence 1   c.   sentence 5
      b.   sentence 4   d.   sentence 6

[1]Two persons seeing each other have a continuous effect on each other's perceptions and expectations of what the other is going to do. [2]Interpersonal communication, then, can be defined broadly as any verbal or nonverbal behavior that is perceived by another person. [3]Communication, in other words, is much more than just the exchange of words. [4]All behavior conveys some message and is, therefore, a form of communication. [5]**Interpersonal communication,** however, is more commonly defined as a message sent by a person to a receiver (or receivers) with the conscious intent of affecting the receiver's behavior. [6]A person sends the message "How are you?" to evoke the response "Fine." [7]A teacher shakes his head to get two students to stop throwing erasers at him. [8]Under this more limited definition, any signal aimed at influencing the receiver's behavior in any way is communication.

—Adapted from Johnson and Johnson, *Joining Together: Group Theory and Group Skills,*
7th ed., p. 142.

_____ 7.   Which sentence is the topic sentence of the paragraph?
   a.   sentence 1   c.   sentence 5
   b.   sentence 3   d.   sentence 7

[1]How do you tell when communication is working effectively and when it is not? [2]What is effective communication? [3]**Effective communication** exists between two persons when the receiver interprets the sender's message in the same way the sender intended it. [4]If John tries to communicate to Jane that it is a wonderful day and he is feeling great by saying "Hi" with a warm smile, and if Jane interprets John's "Hi" as meaning John thinks it is a beautiful day and he is feeling well, then effective communication has taken place. [5]If Jane interprets John's "Hi" as meaning he wants to stop and talk with her, then ineffective communication has taken place.

—Adapted from Johnson & Johnson, *Joining Together: Group Theory and Group Skills,*
7th ed., p. 143.

_____ 8.   Which sentence is the topic sentence of the paragraph?
   a.   sentence 1   c.   sentence 3
   b.   sentence 2   d.   sentence 6

[1]Groups that display a highly cooperative orientation—groups whose members are good listeners, more accepting of the ideas of others, and less possessive of their own ideas—generally demonstrate greater sending and receiving skills. [2]Achievement will be higher in a cooperative group than in a competitive one; more attentiveness will be paid to members' ideas, and a friendlier climate will prevail. [3]A cooperative orientation leads to increased cohesiveness and greater group productivity. [4]Therefore, it can be seen that, one sound means of improving the communication among group members is to increase their cooperativeness and decrease their competitiveness.

—Adapted from Johnson & Johnson, *Joining Together: Group Theory and Group Skills,*
7th ed., p. 143.

_____ 9.   Which sentence is the topic sentence of the paragraph?
   a.   Sentence 1   c.   Sentence 3
   b.   Sentence 2   d.   Sentence 4

[1]Physical factors can also block effective communication within a group. [2]Group members should pay attention to the acoustics of the room in which they are meeting; how members are seated; the duration of the meeting; the ventilation, temperature, and lighting in the room; and what time of day it is. [3]All these are potential physical barriers to effective communication among members. [4]Once noted, of course, they can usually be changed or compensated for.

—Adapted from Johnson and Johnson, *Joining Together: Group Theory and Group Skills,*
7th ed., p. 143.

____ 10. Which sentence is the topic sentence of the paragraph?
  a. sentence 1
  b. sentence 2
  c. sentence 3
  d. sentence 4

Chapter 6: Implied Main Ideas
LAB 6.1 PRACTICE EXERCISE 1

Name _____ Section _____ Date _____ Score (number correct) _____ x 10 = _____

Objective: To use supporting details to determine an implied main idea.

Directions: Read each group of specific details and choose the general idea for each list.

_____ 1. Specific details: cold and snowing, warm and breezy, hot and dry, hot and humid, cool and breezy
   a. seasons
   b. weather conditions
   c. temperature
   d. cloud coverage

_____ 2. Specific details: lipstick, eye shadow, blush, mascara, makeup remover, cotton balls, eyeliner, brushes, face cream
   a. makeup
   b. beauty products
   c. cleansing products for the face
   d. pharmacy aisle

_____ 3. Specific details: skim milk, buttermilk, cottage cheese, string cheese, yoghurt
   a. beverages
   b. cheeses
   c. milk products
   d. diet foods

Directions: Read the following lists of information. Then choose the best statement of the implied main idea for each list.

• Kashada has decided to enroll in college.
• Kashada says she wants to be an elementary teacher.
• She is keeping her part-time job, but she is adjusting her work hours.
• She wants to spend time studying at home and with a study group.
• Kashada wants to have time to meet with her teachers as well.
• By the end of the semester, Kashada plans to have straight A's.

_____ 4. The implied main idea for this list is
   a. Kashada is going to continue working.
   b. Kashada is determined to succeed.
   c. Kashada is going to meet with her teachers.
   d. Kashada is probably a first-generation college student.

- The Roman emperor Nero (A.D. 54-68) demanded that he be worshipped as a god.
- Stating a belief in Jesus as God became a crime against the state.
- Under Nero's rule, a Christian could be pardoned if he or she would burn incense to a Roman god.
- Many Christians who refused to do so were put into prison and tortured.
- Some Christians were nailed to poles, covered with pitch, and set afire.
- These burning human torches lighted Nero's courtyard.

_____ 5. The implied main idea for this list is
   a. People have long suffered for religious reasons.
   b. The emperor Nero wanted to be worshipped.
   c. Many Christians suffered under Nero's rule.
   d. Many Christians have strong faith.

Directions: Read the following paragraphs. Then choose the best statement of the implied main idea for each.

Researchers found that high school students (grades nine to twelve) were much more likely than adults to be familiar with Old Joe the Camel. Old Joe the Camel is a cartoon logo for Camel cigarettes, and young people think of him as a likable figure. In addition, since Old Joe the Camel was first introduced in 1988, Camel cigarettes rose as the choice for smokers under age 18. In fact, since 1988, the number of young smokers who choose Camels has grown from 0.5 percent to 32.8 percent. Children under the age of 18 are thought to be spending $476 million per year on Camel cigarettes, and children make up 25 percent of all Camel sales.

—Adapted from Fishbein and Pease, *The Dynamics of Drug Abuse*, p. 207.

_____ 6. Which statement is the implied main idea?
   a. The cartoon character Old Joe the camel attracted young people to Camel Cigarettes.
   b. Young people should not smoke until they learn the facts.
   c. Camel cigarettes are a favorite brand of cigarettes for many.
   d. Cartoon characters can be used successfully as marketing tools.

Children come into contact with sources of lead during normal indoor and outdoor play. A child can be poisoned from a single high dose of lead or form small amounts taken in over a period of time. In addition, lead can be breathed in. Lead can also be passed from a pregnant mother to her fetus, which can cause low birth weight. Lead can cause damage to the brain, nervous system and kidneys, as well as affect the development of red blood cells. Even at low levels, lead can result in problems with physical coordination, learning, and behavior. Lead is especially dangerous to children under 6 years of age because this is an important time for their growth and development.

—Adapted from Nakamura, *Health in America: A Multicultural Perspective*, p. 196.

_____ 7. Which statement is the implied main idea?
   a. Children are often exposed to many dangers.
   b. Pregnant mothers must be careful to stay away from products with lead.
   c. Chemicals can have many harmful effects on children.
   d. Lead poisoning is a serious danger for children.

For a number of couples, the seeds of divorce already existed when they were dating. In some cases, the dating period was too brief, and the partners did not have time to get to know each other. This is often the case with younger marriages as well as with those who remarry. Such couples may separate rapidly after marriage because they suddenly discover too many differences. The relationship had been brief and easy to end. This is especially true when no children have been born and no joint property has been bought. Lacking a sense of duty to each other, these couples are not as tied to their marriage. Divorce is a fairly easy step, unlikely to have large consequences for them, their families, or society.

—Adapted from Ambert, *Families in the New Millennium*, pp. 374–375.

_____ 8. Which statement is the implied main idea?
   a. Divorce is on the rise.
   b. The reasons people divorce are varied.
   c. Some marriages are doomed from the start and are easily ended.
   d. Successful relationships require more work and compromise.

In his western novel *The Virginian*, written in 1903, Owen Wister described a scene in Wyoming: "We passed the ramparts (walls) of Medicine Bow—thick heaps and fringes of tin cans, and shelving mounds of bottles cast out of saloons." By the 1960s, automobile graveyards marred the beauty of the landscape. Today, disposal of solid waste is a pressing problem in many cities. New York City's only working landfill takes in 25,000 tons of garbage every day, and it will soon be the highest point on the East Cost south of Maine.

—Adapted from Garraty and Carnes, *The American Nation: Volume Two, A History of the United States Since 1865*, 10th ed., p. 914.

_____ 9. Which statement is the implied main idea?
   a. Solid waste disposal is an ongoing and growing problem.
   b.   Wyoming has had environmental problems since the 1900s.
   c. Cities must find ways to manage pollution problems.
   d. New York's geography will soon change as a result of solid waste.

In 1967, the average price of a three-bedroom house was $17,000. A brand-new Cadillac convertible went for $6,700. And a new Volkswagen sold for $1,497. A typewrite cost $39. A man's gray flannel suit could be purchased for $69. A gallon of regular gasoline cost 39 cents. Two decades later, these items rose in price by four times. This sharp rise in price is known as inflation. The rise in inflation started when Lyndon Johnson decided to fight the Vietnam War without raising enough taxes to pay for it. By 1968, the war was costing the United States $3 billion a month. High inflation wiped out many families' savings. It created labor problems when teachers, autoworkers, and others went on strike for higher salaries. They needed higher salaries to keep up with the cost of inflation. For over ten years, family wages remained the same, yet inflation raised the prices of nearly all goods and services. The prices of health care and houses rose far above the rate of inflation. The results were hard on many Americans. Many could not afford health insurance, and there was a sharp rise in homelessness.

—Adapted from Martin et al., *America and Its Peoples: A Mosaic in the Making*, 3rd ed., pp. 1089–90.

_____ 10. Which statement is the implied main idea?
   a. The cost of housing and many other products is continuing to rise.
   b. Inflation has many negative effects.
   c. Many people can't afford health insurance or even homes.
   d. Lyndon Johnson is to be blamed for our high inflation.

78

Chapter 6: Implied Main Ideas
LAB 6.2 PRACTICE EXERCISE 2

Name _____ Section_____ Date_____Score (number correct) _____ x 10 = _____

Objective: To use supporting details to determine an implied main idea.

Directions: Read each group of specific details and choose the general idea for each list.

_____ 1.   Specific details: president, senator, governor, principal, superintendent, CEO, dean
       a.   political leader   c.   business leader
       b.   religious leader   d.   leader

_____ 2.   Specific details: leafy green vegetables, beans, whole-grain cereals, chicken
       a.   ingredients for baking   c.   foods low in fat
       b.   foods for a vegetarian   d.   organic foods

Directions: Read the following lists of information. Then choose the best statement of the implied main idea for each list.

- Jet lag occurs when travelers fly to another time zone and experience fatigue, disorientation, headaches, and other ailments.
- One way to avoid jet lag is to use earphones to listen to music.
- Sleeping with earplugs to block out noise decreases the chances of getting jet lag.
- Some people suggest taking Vitamin B 12 for two weeks, or extra vitamin C, or eating bananas, or drinking orange juice, to replenish potassium and increase energy levels.

_____ 3.   The implied main idea for this list is:
       a.   There are some ways to decrease the effects of jet lag.
       b.   Jet lag is unavoidable and annoying.
       c.   People who like listening to music can avoid jet lag.
       d.   As long as you eat well-balanced meals, you can avoid getting jet lag.

- Benjamin Franklin invented bifocals, the Franklin stove, and a stepladder that converts into a table.
- In his community of Philadelphia, Franklin formed the first volunteer firefighting unit, organized the town watch, and helped form what eventually would become the University of Pennsylvania.
- Franklin signed the Declaration of Independence and was the United States' ambassador to France for many years.
- Though his formal education ended early, Franklin was an avid reader who was interested in many subjects.

_____ 4. The implied main idea for this list is:
    a. Franklin was a busy man but was never president of the United States.
    b. Because he was so talented, Franklin should have become president of the United States.
    c. Benjamin Franklin was a man of many talents.
    d. Franklin could have accomplished more if his formal education had not been cut short.

- Bulldogs appear to be mean and vicious.
- Actually, bulldogs are among the gentlest of breeds.
- Bulldogs were originally bred to fight bulls.
- Through breeding, the savagery in bulldogs was eliminated.

_____ 5. The implied main idea for this list is:
    a. Bulldogs, despite their appearance, are gentle dogs.
    b. Bulldogs are savage and brutal animals.
    c. Bulldogs are strong and agile.
    d. Bulldogs can't be trusted because of their savage natures.

Directions: Read the following paragraphs. Then choose the best statement of the implied main idea for each.

Relationship talk is talking about the nature, quality, direction, or definition of a relationship. Relationship talk is generally considered inappropriate in the early stages of a relationship. A relationship might be prematurely terminated if one partner tries to talk about the relationship too early. Willingness to talk about the relationship is one way to implicitly signal your partner about your level of interest and commitment to the relationship. As relationships move toward greater intimacy, however, the amount of direct relationship talk increases. As the relationship escalates, we should be prepared to discuss our thoughts and feelings about it. In more intimate relationships, relationship talk helps the partners resolve differences in their perceptions of the relationships that might be contributing to conflict and dissatisfaction. Unwillingness to talk about the relationship in an intimate relationship can ultimately drive a partner away.

            — Beebe, Beebe, and Redmond, *Interpersonal Communication: Relating to Others*,
            3rd ed., pp. 336–337.

_____ 6. Which statement is the implied main idea?
    a. It would be a good idea to discuss serious relationship topics on a first date.
    b. Talking about intimate subjects on a first or second date is a good way to determine how serious the other person is about continuing the relationship.
    c. Relationship talk varies as the relationship becomes more intimate.
    d. Partners cannot resolve differences with intimate discussions.

Carcinogens are chemicals or types of radiation that cause cancer. In our society today, the greatest number of cancer cases is thought to result from carcinogens contained in cigarette smoke. Mutagens are chemicals that cause mutations in the DNA of organisms. Some mutagens can lead to severe problems, including cancer and other disorders. Chemicals that cause harm to the unborn are called teratogens. Teratogens that affect the development of human embryos in the womb can cause birth defects. Some toxicants weaken the immune system, reducing the body's ability to defend itself against bacteria, viruses, allergy-causing agents, and other attackers. Still other chemical toxicants, neurotoxins, assault the nervous system. Neurotoxins include various heavy metals such as lead, mercury, and cadmium, as well as pesticides and some chemical weapons developed for use in war.

—Withgott and Brennan, *Environment: The Science behind the Stories*, 3rd ed., pp. 389–390.

_____ 7. Which statement is the implied main idea?
    a. All smoking should be prohibited because of its dangerous effects on health.
    b. Many substances pose health risks to humans living on this planet.
    c. Toxicants can be classified into different types based on their particular effects on health.
    d. Scientists are working to find a cure for cancer and other diseases caused by environmental substances.

The damage to your skin from a single bad sunburn lasts the rest of your life. Even worse, such damage is cumulative. Early signs of sun damage (photodamage) include sunburn, tanning, and increased freckling. Wrinkling, premature aging and age spots, cataracts and other forms of eye damage, sagging of the skin, and the most serious consequence of all—skin cancer—follow these "cute" freckles. If you are an avid sunbather, compare areas such as your hands and face to areas that are almost always covered from the sun's rays. The differences that you see are usually the result of sun exposure over time.

—Adapted from Donatelle, *Access to Health*, 10th ed., p. 496.

_____ 8. Which statement is the implied main idea?
    a. Tanning should be avoided because of the harm caused by the sun's rays.
    b. The long-term effects of sun exposure can be quite harmful.
    c. Sun exposure causes the skin to age prematurely.
    d. Freckling of the skin is actually a sign of sun damage that can even lead to skin cancer.

When AOL.com announced that it was introducing a music service to its subscribers based on MusicNet, a consortium of music labels offering a music catalog of 250,000 songs, the company earned instant credibility because of the reputation of its partners and the size of the catalog assets. Similarly, when Steven Jobs, CEO and founder of Apple Computer, announced iTunes, a new service offering legal, downloadable individual song tracks for 99 cents a tune that would be playable on Apple iPods or Apple desktops, the company was given better than average odds of success simply because of Apple's prior success with innovative hardware designs and the large stable of music labels which Apple had lined up to support its online music catalog of over four million titles. Few competitors could match the combination of cheap, legal songs and powerful hardware to play them on.

—Adapted from Laudon and Traver, *E-commerce,* 3rd ed., pp. 64–65.

_____ 9. What is the topic of this passage?
    a. Apple Computer company
    b. AOL.com
    c. downloading music from the Internet
    d. the competitive advantage of prior success

___ 10. What is the implied main idea?
   a. Music can be downloaded from the Internet if the user has access to music-players.
   b. Businesses can build large global markets for music on the Internet.
   c. Successful companies such as Aol.com and Apple Computer already had a competitive edge when starting a music downloading venture.
   d. Downloading music illegally from the Internet is the same as stealing.

Chapter 6: Implied Main Ideas
LAB 6.3 REVIEW TEST 1

Name _____ Section _____ Date _____ Score (number correct) _____ x 10 = _____

Directions: Read each group of specific details and choose the general idea for each list.

____ 1. Specific details: tutoring, counseling, advising, writing lab, math lab, academic computer center
   a. community services
   b. business resources
   c. student support services
   d. career services

____ 2. Specific details: hood, zipper, sleeves, pockets, down lining
   a. blouse   c. vest
   b. T-shirt   d. winter jacket

Directions: Read the following lists of information. Then choose the best statement of the implied main idea for each list.

- In 1832, Abraham Lincoln ran for state office and lost.
- In 1843, Lincoln ran for Congress and lost.
- In 1854, Lincoln ran for a seat in the U.S. Senate and lost.
- After later winning seats in the state legislature, U.S. Congress, and U. S. Senate, Lincoln ran for president of the United States in 1860 and won.

____ 3. The implied main idea for this list is
   a. Lincoln continued his political career despite some setbacks.
   b. Lincoln should never have run for public office.
   c. Lincoln was a leader many people did not like.
   d. Abraham Lincoln never had to do hard physical work.

- A female praying mantis often mates with a male and then devours it.
- Female lightning bugs have been known to use a different light pattern to lure a male only to destroy it.
- Black widow spiders mate and then kill the male.
- Swordtail fish mothers must be separated from their newborns to prevent the mother fish from eating the babies.

____ 4. The implied main idea for this list is
   a. There are always surprises in nature.
   b. Females in nature are not always nurturing and kind.
   c. Spiders are dangerous.
   d. Insects have many traits similar to humans.

Directions: Read the following paragraphs. Then choose the best statement of the implied main idea for each.

Listening skills are crucial for developing and maintaining relationships. Listening clues you in to others' needs, wants, and values, and it enables you to respond to them in appropriate ways. In the initial stages of a relationship, partners share a great deal of information. The amount of information tapers off in the later stages as a relationship continues over time. This tapering off creates the illusion that you don't have to listen as much or as well as you did early on. But listening is a way to demonstrate ongoing interest in another person. Even in long-term relationships, you do not know everything your partner has to say. It is still important to stop, look, and listen—to put down the newspaper or turn off the radio when your close friend begins talking to you.
— Beebe, Beebe, and Redmond, *Interpersonal Communication:Relating to Others*, 3rd ed., p. 337.

_____ 5. Which statement is the implied main idea?
   a. Couples who have been together a long time do not need to listen as much or as well to each other as they did when the relationship was in the early stages.
   b. Everyone needs good listening skills to nurture and maintain good relationships.
   c. People who do not listen well are selfish people.
   d. Couples who are in long-term relationships learn to read each other's minds.

Most couples spend little time before their wedding day reflecting on the decision to marry. Many young people believe that a couple's satisfaction increases through the first year of marriage. They also believe that the best single predictor of marital satisfaction is the quality of a couple's sex life. Furthermore, many endorse the belief that "If my spouse loves me, he or she should instinctively know what I want and need to be happy." Often young couples feel that no matter how they behave, their spouses should love them simply because they are married. Consequently, many couples are disappointed, and their marriages become less satisfying and more conflict-ridden as these ideas are proven wrong.

—Adapted from Berk, *Development Through the Lifespan,* 4th ed., p. 477.

_____ 6. Which statement is the implied main idea?
   a. Many young people have a mythical image of marriage that is not based on reality.
   b. The first year of marriage is usually the best one.
   c. Couples should agree to always agree with one another.
   d. Most couples should wait several years for marriage in order to have a better chance of staying together in the long run.

Any money contributed by your employer to your retirement fund is like extra income paid to you beyond your salary. This is referred to as a defined-contribution plan. In addition, having such a retirement account can encourage you to save money each pay period by directing a portion of your income to the account before you receive your paycheck. Investing in a defined-contribution plan also offers tax benefits. The retirement account allows you to defer taxes on income paid by your employer because your contribution to your account is deducted from your pay before taxes are taken out. Also, the income generated by your investments in a retirement account is not taxed until you withdraw the money after you retire. This tax benefit is very valuable because it provides you with more money that can be invested and accumulated. In addition, by the time you are taxed on the investments (at retirement), you will likely be in a lower tax bracket because you will have less income.

—Adapted from Madura, *Personal Finance,* 3rd ed., pp. 558–559.

_____ 7. Which statement is the implied main idea?
   a. Most people will be in a lower tax bracket by retirement age because they will have less income.
   b. A defined-contribution retirement plan provides many benefits for employees.
   c. Defined-contribution plans have become very popular because employers are required to contribute to their employees' retirement funds.
   d. Even if Social Security pays retirement benefits, many people will want more income after retirement than it provides.

Life inside prison is different—very different—from life outside prison. It is not uncommon that inmates are injured by violence while imprisoned, whether it is caused by correctional staff, other inmates, or accidents. Sexual violence in prison has become a national concern as well. Some inmates who claim they have been raped in prison state that they were considered the "property" of prison gangs and would be bartered for money or favors. Prison gangs, known as security-risk groups, pose another serious problem in prisons. For example, Rikers Island in New York has identified 44 security risk groups that operate within the prison. Health is an additional issue. The health of the average 50-year-old prisoner approximates that of the average 60-year-old person in the free community. Sexually transmitted diseases, including HIV/AIDS and other communicable diseases, pose serious challenges to administrators of both adult and juvenile justice systems. In 2002, the overall rate of confirmed AIDS cases among the nation's prison populations was 3 ½ times the rate in the U.S. general population. Finally, nearly one in five inmates in U.S. prisons reports having a mental illness. According to one report, "Jails have become the poor person's mental hospitals."

—Adapted from Fagin, *Criminal Justice,* 2nd ed., pp. 501–507.

_____ 8. What is the topic of this passage?
   a. gang violence in prisons
   b. need for prison reform
   c. difficulties of prison life
   d. mental health issues of prisoners

_____ 9. What kind of details are contained in the passage?
   a. a list of reasons explaining the need for prison reform
   b. the causes of our high crime rate
   c. examples of bad prisons
   d. a list of problems experienced by prisoners

_____ 10. What is the implied main idea?
   a. Drugs and gang violence are filling our prisons, causing problems associated with over-crowded conditions.
   b. Because problems in prisons are increasing, the entire prison system is in need of reform.
   c. The number of prisoners is increasing due to federal drug prosecutions, firearms violations, and mandatory sentencing.
   d. The physical and mental health of inmates is a serious issue for prisoners, the prison system, and the community.

85

Chapter 6: Implied Main Ideas
LAB 6.4 REVIEW TEST 2

Name _____ Section _____ Date _____ Score (number correct) _____ x 10 = _____

Directions: Read each group of specific details and choose the general idea for each list.

_____ 1. Specific details: actors, director, producer, editor, make-up artist, lighting technician
  a. the movies
  b. people needed to make a movie
  c. people who live in Hollywood
  d. creative people

_____ 2. Specific details: ammonia, bleach, detergent, wax, polish, soap, degreaser
  a. items used to clean
  b. items stored in a cabinet
  c. items used to sterilize
  d. items found in a store

Directions: Read the following lists of information. Then choose the best statement of the implied main idea for each list.

- Car crashes are the leading cause of death for people between the ages of 13 and 19.
- According to experts, between 1988 and 1998, more than 65,000 teenagers died in car wrecks.
- Many teens are involved in car wrecks because of a lack of driving experience.
- Experts say that most of these fatal car crashes were the result of "driver error."
- Inexperienced teenage drivers are easily distracted while they are behind the wheel.

_____ 3. The implied main idea for this list is
  a. There are many dangers for teenage drivers.
  b. Young drivers lack experience.
  c. Lack of experience leads to high death rates for young drivers.
  d. The driving age for teenagers should be moved to eighteen years of age.

- Set your financial goals for when you retire.
- Estimate how much money you will need upon retirement.
- Estimate you income at retirement.
- Calculate the difference between your estimated need and your estimated income.
- Determine how much you must save annually between now and retirement.

_____ 4. The implied main idea for this list is
  a. Too many people retire without a plan.
  b. Today's workers will have reduced future benefits for retirement.
  c. Most people do not have enough money to support themselves when they retire.
  d. Planning for retirement involves several steps.

Directions: Read the following paragraphs. Then choose the best statement of the implied main idea for each.

Many people think there is something "natural" about gender distinctions because biology does make one sex different from the other. But we must be careful not to think of social differences in biological terms. In 1848, for example, women were denied the vote because many people assumed that women did not have enough intelligence or interest in politics. Such attitudes had nothing to do with biology. Another example is athletic performance. In 1925, most people believed that the best women runners could never compete with men in a marathon. Today, the fastest women routinely post better times than the fastest men of decades past.

—Adapted from Macionis, *Sociology*, 13th ed., p. 328

_____ 5. Which statement is the implied main idea?
   a. Men are naturally better at physical competition than women.
   b. Women are just as smart as men.
   c. Most of the difference between men and women turn out to be socially created.
   d. Attitude is often more important than ability.

Exercise can help keep a woman physically fit during pregnancy. In addition, exercise is a great mood booster, helping women feel more in control of their changing bodies and reducing postpartum depression. Expending additional energy through exercise will also allow intake of compensatory energy when a ravenous appetite kicks in. Moreover, regular moderate exercise will reduce the risk of gestational diabetes, help keep blood pressure down, and confer all the cardiovascular benefits that it does for nonpregnant individuals. Regular exercise can also shorten the duration of active labor. Finally, a woman who keeps fit during pregnancy will have an easier time resuming a fitness routine and losing weight after pregnancy.

— Thompson and Manore, *Nutrition for Life*, 2nd ed., p. 346.

_____ 6. Which statement is the implied main idea?
   a. Women have many challenges to face while pregnant.
   b. Regular exercise has many benefits for women who are pregnant.
   c. Maintaining an exercise program is necessary in order to lose weight.
   d. Regular moderate exercise has many health benefits.

Cigarette smoking can delay fetal growth and may contribute to spontaneous abortions. Babies born to mothers who abuse alcohol may have fetal alcohol syndrome. These babies may have heart defects, limb abnormalities, and delays in motor and language development. Cocaine and heroin use during pregnancy can kill a fetus or cause abnormalities. The use of marijuana is associated with poor fetal weight gain and behavioral abnormalities in the newborn.

—Adapted from Johnson, *Human Biology: Concepts and Current Issues*, 5th ed., p. 419.

_____ 7. Which statement is the implied main idea?
   a. There are many dangerous substances that can physically harm a fetus and have damaging effects on a newborn.
   b. Mothers who have abused drugs should never have children.
   c. Cigarette smoking should be banned in all public areas because of the dangers of cigarette smoke to newborn babies.
   d. Society will have to foot the bill for children born to mothers who abused drugs and alcohol.

87

College students under stress can have physical problems that include unusual fatigue, sleeping problems, frequent colds, and even chest pains and nausea. Students under stress may even behave differently. They may pace the floor, eat too much, cry a lot, smoke and drink more than usual, or physically strike out at others by hitting or throwing things. Emotionally, students under stress experience anxiety, depression, fear and irritability, as well as anger and frustration. Mental symptoms of stress include problems in concentration, memory, and decision making. Students under stress even lose their sense of humor often.

—Adapted from Ciccarelli and White, *Psychology*, 2nd ed., p. 433.

_____ 8. Which statement is the implied main idea?
   a. College puts most students under too much pressure.
   b. College students need counseling in order to handle the stress of difficult classes.
   c. Stress in college students can show itself in many ways.
   d. Most people experience some degree of stress on a daily basis.

The newest role for genetic counselors involves testing people to identify whether they are susceptible to future disorders because of genetic abnormalities. For instance, Huntington's disease typically does not appear until people reach their 40s. However, genetic testing can identify much earlier whether a person carries the flawed gene that produces Huntington's disease. Although such testing may bring welcome relief if the results are negative, positive results, however, may produce just the opposite effect. Some people who discover they carry the flawed gene might well experience depression and remorse. In fact, some studies show that 10% of people who find they have the flawed gene that leads to Huntington's disease never recover fully on an emotional level. So, is it better to know, or not?

—Adapted from Feldman, *Child Development*, 5th ed., p. 54.

_____ 9. Which statement is the implied main idea?
   a. People who suspect they might have a future illness will find relief from worry with genetic testing.
   b. Genetic testing helps people prepare for a future illness.
   c. Most people can't face the results of genetic testing.
   d. Genetic testing raises difficult practical and ethical questions.

Charles Chatman was exonerated from prison last month by DNA testing while serving a 99-year sentence for sexual assault. Last week, two men were cleared of separate murder convictions in Mississippi after new DNA testing led authorities to another man now charged in both slayings. Since 1989, there have been 213 post-conviction DNA exonerations in the United States. Of those, 149 came in the past seven years. In Virginia, officials are conducting a sweeping examination of more than 534,000 files, the largest such review in U.S. history. Three years and five exonerations after the effort began, authorities have identified 2, 215 more cases they say are worthy of scrutiny.

—Adapted from Schmalleger, *Criminal Justice: A Brief Introduction*, 8th. ed., p.341.

_____ 10. Which statement is the implied main idea?
   a. The justice system clearly does not work as innocent people are being sent to jail.
   b. DNA testing is helping many wrongfully-accused prisoners prove their innocence.
   c. Most prisoners are probably innocent of the crimes for which they were convicted.
   d. Claims of innocence are almost always supported by DNA testing.

Chapter 6: Implied Main Ideas
LAB 6.5 MASTERY TEST 1

Name _____ Section _____ Date _____ Score (number correct) _____ x 10 = _____

Directions: Read each group of specific details and choose the general idea for each list.

_____ 1. Specific details: ads, articles, glossy photos, recipes, make-up advice
    a. items in a magazine
    b. parts of a newspaper
    c. a poster
    d. part of a letter

_____ 2. Specific details: keyboard, monitor, mouse, speakers, mouse pad
    a. a rodent
    b. a television
    c. an electronic piano
    d. a computer

Directions: Read the following lists of information. Then choose the best statement of the implied main idea for each list.

- Chocolate comes from cacao beans.
- The word cacao means "bitter juice."
- The word chocolate means "sour water. "
- Baking chocolate is a bitter ingredient used for cooking.

_____ 3. The implied main idea for this list is:
    a. Chocolate is a worldwide favorite.
    b. Chocolate has existed for many years.
    c. Chocolate is not sweet in its raw form.
    d. Many people enjoy chocolate candy.

- Koy Detmer, a backup quarterback for the Philadelphia Eagles, buys a new traveling outfit for less than $100 at the beginning of each season at Wal-Mart.
- Detmer travels with only a toothbrush and his playbook.
- When he leaves each game to get on the plane, he puts the playbook in a box to travel with the team.
- The only thing he travels with on his way home is the toothbrush in his pocket.

_____ 4. The implied main idea for this list is:
    a. Professional quarterbacks are very unusual.
    b. Professional backup quarterbacks do not make much money.
    c. Koy Detmer has unusual traveling habits.
    d. Football players are very superstitious athletes.

Directions: Read the following paragraphs. Then choose the best statement of the implied main idea for each.

To be genuine means that you honestly seek to be yourself rather than someone you are not. It also means taking an honest interest in others and considering the uniqueness of each individual and situation, avoiding generalizations or strategies that focus only on your own needs and desires. A manipulative person has hidden agendas; a genuine person uses words to discuss issues and problems openly and honestly.

—Beebe, Beebe, and Redmond, *Interpersonal Communication:Relating to Others*, 3rd ed., p. 192.

_____ 5. Which statement is the implied main idea?
a. People who think of other people's interests tend to be more honest and genuine and discuss issues openly.
b. Someone with a hidden agenda would be interested in the interests of others.
c. In communication, it is important to determine if a person is being honest.
d. If you are not comfortable with yourself, you should try to change.

Federal judges are not elected and are almost impossible to remove. Indeed, their social backgrounds probably make the courts the most elite-dominated policymaking institution. If democracy requires that key policymakers always be elected or be continually responsible to those who are, then the courts diverge sharply from these requirements. Interest groups can effectively use the courts to achieve their policy goals. Some critics see the courts as too powerful for their own—or the nation's—good. Some question the qualifications of judges for making policy decisions and balancing interests.

—Adapted from Edwards, Wattenberg, and Lineberry, *Government in America: People, Politics, and Policy,* 12th ed., pp. 531–534.

_____ 6. Which statement is the implied main idea?
a. The federal court system is corrupt.
b. Interest groups have powerful influence in the federal court system.
c. In some ways, the courts are not a very democratic institution.
d. Judges are not necessarily qualified to rule on decisions of national policy.

The war against Troy was fought as part of the expansion and unification of Greece, but Homer tells it as if it were the consequence of a conflict among the Olympian gods and goddesses. The Trojan War erupted over a dispute over which of three goddesses was the most beautiful: Athena, goddess of wisdom; Aphrodite, goddess of love; or Hera, queen of the gods and wife of Zeus, king of the gods. According to legend, the war ended after ten years of hard fighting, and only then through trickery. The Greeks built a huge wooden horse, left it as a peace offering on the beach before Troy, and departed in their ships. The horse, however, was only a ruse, as Greek soldiers were hiding inside it. After the horse was taken into Troy, the Greeks crept out in the middle of the night and opened the gates of the city to the army waiting outside.

—Adapted from Janaro and Altshuler, *The Art of Being Human,* 8th ed., p. 105.

_____ 7. Which statement is the implied main idea?
a. The Trojan War lasted ten years.
b. The Trojan War did not really happen.
c. History is often told in the form of stories.
d. Trickery is often used to settle disputes.

There are two ways we share feelings with our partners. The first includes disclosing information about our past or current emotional status, such as sadness about the death of a family member or fear about what we will do after we graduate. The second way we share emotions is the direct expression of emotions, such as expressing attraction, love, or disappointment toward our partner. As relationships become more intimate, we have a greater expectation that our partner will disclose emotions openly. The amount of risk associated with such emotional disclosures varies from person to person. Most of us are comfortable sharing positive emotions such as happiness and joy, but we are more reserved about sharing negative emotions such as fear or disappointment. We may think expressing negative emotions makes us appear weak or vulnerable. However, in a study of forty-six committed, romantic couples, researchers found that the number one problem was the inability to talk about negative feelings. For example, partners often made the following types of observations: "When she gets upset, she stops talking"; "He never lets me know when he's upset with something he doesn't like"; and "He just silently pouts." We generally want to know how our partners in intimate relationships are feeling, even if those feelings are negative.

— Beebe, Beebe, and Redmond, *Interpersonal Communication: Relating to Others*, 3rd ed., p. 336.

_____ 8. What is the topic of this passage?
   a. romantic relationships
   b. negative feelings
   c. communication problems
   d. sharing feelings with partners

_____ 9. What kind of details are contained in the passage?
   a. examples of issues that cause problems in relationships
   b. steps toward building a healthy relationship
   c. reasons for partner counseling
   d. a description of the ways partners share feelings

_____ 10. What is the implied main idea?
   a. Couples in strong, healthy relationships risk sharing and expressing both positive and negative feelings in order to achieve effective communication.
   b. The number one communication problem among couples is the inability to discuss negative feelings.
   c. Sharing negative feelings is a sign of weakness.
   d. Sharing emotions and expressing feelings require no risk.

Name _____ Section _____ Date _____ Score (number correct) _____ x 10 = _____

Directions: Read each group of specific details and choose the general idea for each list.

____ 1. Specific details: croutons, lettuce, tomatoes, cheese, turkey slices, sliced hard-boiled eggs, salad dressing
   a. turkey sandwich   c. food
   b chef salad   d. lunch

____ 2. Specific details: fingerprints, a dead body, a recently fired gun
   a. crime   c. murder
   b. clues at a crime scene d. investigation

____ 3. Specific details: shovels, hammers, fertilizer, grass seed, nails
   a. tools   c. items for lawn care
   b. items to build with   d. items in a hardware store

Directions: Read the following lists of information. Then choose the best statement of the implied main idea for each list.

- A smooth golf ball will travel about 110 yards.
- A dimpled golf ball will travel about 250 yards.
- Dimples first appeared on golf balls about 100 years ago.
- A dimpled golf ball will travel higher and faster than a smooth golf ball.

____ 4. The implied main idea for this list is:
   a. Golf is a game of strategy and timing.
   b. Golf equipment is important to winning the game.
   c. The dimples on a golf ball improve its ability to travel at a greater distance.
   d. It was harder to win at golf 100 years ago.

- Buzzing insects such as flies or mosquitoes make their noise by the rapid movement of their wings.
- Cicadas make a noise with the rapid movement in a tambourine-like structure in their abdomen.
- Crickets rub one wing against the other.
- Humans use their voices to make sounds.

____ 5. The implied main idea for this list is:
   a. All insects use the same procedure to make sounds.
   b. Insects, like humans, use their voices to make sounds.
   c. Unlike humans, who have voices, insects have other methods of making sounds.
   d. Insects are annoying when they make noises, and they are not really talking to each   other.

Directions: Read the following paragraphs. Then choose the best statement of the implied main idea for each

On September 11, 2001, terrorist attacks on the World Trade Center in New York and the Pentagon in Washington killed thousands and exposed the nation's vulnerability to unconventional attacks. Communism was no longer the principal threat to the security of the United States, and our foreign policy goals suddenly changed to ending terrorism. At the same time, a number of critical areas of the world, such as the Middle East and the India-Pakistan border, exhibited a frightening tendency to conflict.

—Adapted from Edwards, Wattenberg, and Lineberry, *Government in America: People, Politics, and Policy,* 12th ed., pp. 612–613.

_____ 6. Which statement is the implied main idea?
   a. Suddenly the world seems a more threatening place.
   b. The United States is no longer the world's only superpower.
   c. The role of the national government is to help other countries.
   d. America is no longer safe.

The most satisfying relationships are those in which both partners refrain from continually disagreeing, criticizing, and making negative comments to each other. Both individuals learn to accept the other and do not feel compelled to continually point out flaws or failures. One study found that well-adjusted couples focus their complaints on specific behaviors, whereas maladjusted couples complain about each other's personal characteristics. Well-adjusted couples are also kinder and more positive and have more humor in their interactions. They tend to agree with each other's complaints, whereas the partners in maladjusted relationships launch counter-complaints. In addition, happy couples, when compared to unhappy couples, display more affection through positive nonverbal cues, display more supportive behaviors, and make more attempts to avoid conflicts.

— Beebe, Beebe, and Redmond, *Interpersonal Communication: Relating to Others*, 3rd ed., p. 341.

_____ 7. Which statement is the implied main idea?
   a. A good relationship establishes the need to continually disagree and the freedom to make frequent negative comments to each other.
   b. Well-adjusted couples use humor and share complaints in a positive and supportive manner.
   c. To communicate well, couples should avoid using nonverbal cues.
   d. To communicate well, couples should never avoid conflicts.

93

Psychologists can teach people to harness psychological forces to eliminate unhealthy behaviors such as smoking and initiate healthy behaviors such as regular exercise. Parents can learn parenting practices to maintain solid bonds with their children. Knowledge of psychology can also help eliminate forces that make strangers reluctant to offer assistance in emergency situations.

—Adapted from Gerrig and Zimbardo, *Psychology and Life,* 18th ed., p. 8.

_____ 8. Which statement is the implied main idea?
   a. Strangers are often afraid of interfering during emergency situations.
   b. People with unhealthy habits can't improve their lives on their own.
   c. Parenting is a skill that can be learned.
   d. Psychologists have devised many strategies to help people gain control over problematic aspects of their lives.

Like solar power, wind produces no emissions once the necessary equipment is manufactured and installed. As a replacement for fossil fuel combustion in the average U.S. utility generator, scientists have calculated that a wind turbine can prevent the release of more than 1,500 tons of carbon dioxide, 6.5 tons of sulfur dioxide, 3.2 tons of nitrogen oxides, and 60 pounds of mercury in a year. The amount of carbon pollution that all U.S. wind turbines together prevent from entering the atmosphere is greater than the cargo of a 50-car freight train, with each car holding 100 tons of solid carbon, each and every day. One recent study found that wind turbines produce 23 times more energy than they consume. Another societal benefit of wind power is that farmers and ranchers can lease their land for wind development, which provides them extra revenue while also increasing property tax income for rural communities.

_____ 9. What is the topic of this passage?
   a. air pollution
   b. wind power
   c. energy consumption
   d. relief for farmers

_____ 10. What is the implied main idea?
   a. Air pollution is a major problem in an energy-driven country.
   b. The United States consumes more energy than any other country in the world.
   c. Wind power has many benefits.
   d. Scientists are searching for alternate energy sources.

Chapter 7: Supporting Details, Outlines, and Concept Maps
LAB 7.1 PRACTICE EXERCISE 1

Name _____ Section _____ Date _____ Score (number correct) _____ x 10 = _____

Objective: To identify major and minor details.

Directions: Read each passage and answer the questions that follow.

A. [1]Nearly 4 million Americans have Alzheimer's disease, including the late former President Ronald Reason. [2]Alzheimer's disease is the most common type of dementia found in adults and the elderly. [3]It has also become the third leading cause of death in late adulthood. [4]Only heart disease and cancer are responsible for more deaths.

[5]There is at present no cure, but in recent years several new medications have been developed that seem to slow the progress of the disease. [6]One common treatment is to place the person on a drug which blocks the breakdown of acetylcholine. [7]This is the neurotransmitter involved in the formation of memories. [8]Other drugs to reduce the agitation, restlessness, and hallucinations that can come with the disease may be administered. [9]There is some evidence that taking an herbal supplement, gingko biloba, may help the memory problems of some Alzheimer's victims. [10]This supplement, however, has shown not to affect the functioning of normal memory.

—Adapted from Ciccarelli and White, *Psychology*, 2nd ed., p. 255.

_____1. Sentence 2 is a _____.
   a. main idea
   b. major supporting detail
   c. minor supporting detail

_____2. Sentence 3 is a _____.
   a. main idea
   b. major supporting detail
   c. minor supporting detail

_____3. Sentence 5 is a _____.
   a. main idea
   b. major supporting detail
   c. minor supporting detail

_____4. Sentence 6 is a _____.
   a. main idea
   b. major supporting detail
   c. minor supporting detail

_____5. Sentence 7 is a _____.
   a. main idea
   b. major supporting detail
   c. minor supporting detail

B. [1]Labels, ranging from simple tags attached to products to complex graphics that are part of the package, perform several functions. [2]At the very least, the label identifies the product or brand. [3]The name Sunkist stamped on oranges is one perfect example of this. [4]The label might also describe several things about the product—who made it, where it was made, when it was made, its contents, how it is to be used, and how to use it safely. [5]Finally, the label might help to promote the brand, support its positioning, and connect with customers. [6]For example, Pepsi recently re-crafted the graphics on its soft drink cans as part of a broader effort to give the brand more meaning and social relevance to its youth audience.

—Adapted from Kotler and Armstrong, *Principles of Marketing*, 13th ed., p. 232.

_____6. Sentence 1 is a _____.
   a. main idea
   b.   major supporting detail
   c. minor supporting detail

_____7. Sentence 2 is a _____.
   a. main idea
   b. major supporting detail
   c. minor supporting detail

_____8. Sentence 3 is a _____.
   a. main idea
   b. major supporting detail
   c. minor supporting detail

_____9. Sentence 5 is a _____.
   a. main idea
   b. major supporting detail
   c. minor supporting detail

_____10. Sentence 6 is a _____.
   a. main idea
   b. major supporting detail
   c. minor supporting detail

Name _____ Section_____ Date _____Score (number correct) _____ x 10 = _____

Objective: To identify major and minor details.

Directions: After reading the paragraph below, answer the following questions.

Red Light Photo Enforcement

[1]Currently, some large cities are using a new technology called Red Light Photo Enforcement (Photo Red), a camera-monitored red light, for several reasons. [2]First, Photo Red is an advantage for the citizens. [3]The presence of a camera to capture the license plate of vehicles that run a red light will reduce the number of crashes at a busy intersection. [4]For example, in one study, the number of accidents was reduced by 40% because it produced generalized changes in driver behavior. [5]In that same study, researchers reported that drivers at nearby intersections also stopped more at red lights. [6]Another advantage to the citizens is that the technology is more equitable, or fair. [7]Usually at the busiest of intersections, several vehicles run the red light consecutively. [8]A police officer must decide which car—the first, the second, or the third—should be stopped. [9]With Photo Red, all drivers of any vehicles with visible license plates that run the red light will be ticketed. [10]Second, the use of camera-monitored red lights is an advantage for the police officers. [11]Photo Red will prevent officers from having to risk their lives by venturing into a busy intersection to apprehend a motorist. In addition, the technology will allow officers to focus on other criminal activity in the city.

_____ 1. Sentence 1 is a
   a. main idea.
   b. major supporting detail.
   c. minor supporting detail.

_____ 2. Sentence 2 is a
   a. main idea.
   b. major supporting detail.
   c. minor supporting detail.

_____ 3. Sentence 3 is a
   a. main idea.
   b. major supporting detail.
   c. minor supporting detail.

_____ 4. Sentence 4 is a
   a. main idea.
   b. major supporting detail.
   c. minor supporting detail.

_____ 5. Sentence 10 is a
   a. main idea.
   b. major supporting detail.
   c. minor supporting detail.

[1]Many citizens have concerns about Photo Red and are reluctant to allow the technology in their city. [2]For one, they worry that they will be punished if someone else is driving their car when the vehicle is photographed. [3]However, if a motorist signs an affidavit that attests that a friend or relative was driving the car, then the ticket will go to that driver. [4]Another concern is that the presence of a camera is allowing "Big Brother" into their lives and will be an infringement of their privacy and civil rights. [5]In California, for example, the camera actually photographs the driver's face as well as the license plate. [6]However, proponents of the technology argue that driving is a privilege, and other motorists have the right to be safe on the roads. [7]The technology, they argue, is there to ensure the rights of the citizens, not to take it away. [8]A final concern is that the cost of the technology will require an increase in citizens' taxes, but the cost is minimal. [9]In Virginia Beach, Virginia, for instance, the cost for one year is paid for in the fines incurred by 3.5 tickets a day. [10]Currently, they are issuing 16 tickets a day at one Photo Red intersection, which is more than enough to cover the expense.

_____ 6. Sentence 1 is a
   a. main idea.
   b. major supporting detail.
   c. minor supporting detail.

_____ 7. Sentence 2 is a
   a. main idea.
   b. major supporting detail.
   c. minor supporting detail.

_____ 8. Sentence 4 is a
   a. main idea.
   b. major supporting detail.
   c. minor supporting detail.

_____ 9. Sentence 5 is a
   a. main idea.
   b. major supporting detail.
   c. minor supporting detail.

_____ 10. Sentence 8 is a
   a. main idea.
   b. major supporting detail.
   c. minor supporting detail.

Name _____ Section _____ Date _____ Score (number correct) _____ x 10 = _____

Directions: Read each paragraph and answer the questions that follow.

[1]For most species, a high intensity of hunting or harvesting by humans will not in itself pose a threat of extinction, but for some species it can. [2]The Siberian tiger is one such species. [3]Large in size, few in number, long-lived, and raising few young in its lifetime, the Siberian tiger is just the type of animal to be vulnerable to population reduction by hunting. [4]The advent of Russian hunting nearly drove the animal extinct, whereas decreased hunting during and after World War II allowed a population increase. [5]Over the past century, hunting has led to steep declines in the populations of many other animals. [6]The Atlantic gray whale has gone extinct, and several other whales remain threatened or endangered. [7]Gorillas and other primates that are killed for their meat may face extinction soon. [8]Thousands of sharks are killed each year simply for their fins, which are used in soup. [9]Today the oceans contain only 10% of the large animals they once did.

—Adapted from Withgott and Brennan, *Environment: The Science Behind the Stories*, 3rd ed., pp. 307–308.

_____ 1. Sentence 1 is a
   a. main idea.
   b. major supporting detail.
   c. minor supporting detail.

_____ 2. Sentence 2 is a
   a. main idea.
   b. major supporting detail.
   c. minor supporting detail.

_____ 3. Sentence 3 is a
   a. main idea.
   b. major supporting detail.
   c. minor supporting detail.

_____ 4. Sentence 7 is a
   a. main idea.
   b. major supporting detail.
   c. minor supporting detail.

_____ 5. Sentence 9 is a
   a. main idea.
   b. major supporting detail.
   c. minor supporting detail.

[1]You've heard the claims: "Lose weight while you sleep. [2]Lose 30 pounds in 30 days. [3]Eat anything you want and still lose weight." [4]However, products and programs that promise quick and easy weight loss are bogus. [5]Reaching and maintaining a healthy weight are based on three basic facts. [6]First, to lose weight, you have to lower your intake of calories and increase your physical activity. [7]Second, the faster you lose weight, the more likely you'll gain it back. [8]Experts recommend a goal of about a pound a week. [9]Third, to maintain weight loss, health experts suggest that you eat nutritious foods, cut your intake of calories and exercise more. [10]Be skeptical about products that claim they will keep weight off you permanently.

— "Amazing Claims." Federal Trade Commission, 14 September 2004

_____ 6. Sentence 1 is a
     a. main idea.
     b. major supporting detail.
     c. minor supporting detail.

_____ 7. Sentence 5 is a
     a. main idea.
     b. major supporting detail.
     c. minor supporting detail.

_____ 8. Sentence 6 is a
     a. main idea.
     b. major supporting detail.
     c. minor supporting detail.

_____ 9. Sentence 7 is a
     a. main idea.
     b. major supporting detail.
     c. minor supporting detail.

_____ 10. Sentence 8 is a
     a. main idea.
     b. major supporting detail.
     c. minor supporting detail.

Name _____ Section _____ Date _____ Score (number correct) _____ x 10 = _____

Directions: Read each passage and answer the questions that follow.

A. [1]One approach to friendship argues that friendships are maintained by rules. [2]When these rules are followed, the friendship is strong and mutually satisfying. [3]For example, the rules for keeping a friendship call for such behaviors as standing up for your friend in his or her absence, sharing information and feelings about successes, demonstrating emotional support for a friend, trusting and offering to help a friend in need, an trying to make a friend happy when you're together. [4]On the other hand, when these rules are broken, the friendship suffers and may die. [5]A friendship is likely to be in trouble when one or both friends are intolerant of the other's friends, discuss confidences with third parties, fail to demonstrate positive support, nag, and/or fail to trust or confide in the other.

—Adapted from DeVito, *The Interpersonal Communication Book*, 12th ed., p. 219.

_____ 1. Sentence 1 is a _____.
   a. main idea
   b. major supporting detail
   c. minor supporting detail

_____ 2. Sentence 2 is a _____.
   a. main idea
   b. major supporting detail
   c. minor supporting detail

_____ 3. Sentence 3 is a _____.
   a. main idea
   b. major supporting detail
   c. minor supporting detail

_____ 4. Sentence 4 is a _____.
   a. main idea
   b. major supporting detail
   c. minor supporting detail

_____ 5. Sentence 5 is a _____.
   a. main idea
   b. major supporting detail
   c. minor supporting detail

B. [1]"A Mind is a Terrible Thing to Waste." [2]"Friends Don't Let Friends Drive Drunk." [3]We have all benefited from public service announcements, defined as messages on behalf of some good cause. [4]A leader in creating these announcements is the Ad Council, a private nonprofit organization whose mission is to identify a select number of significant public issues and stimulate action. [5]The Ad Council often teams up with government agencies or nonprofit organizations to get a message out to the public. [6]For example, currently the Ad Council and the U.S. Department of Health and Human Services have a joint campaign to inspire healthier lifestyles. [7]One of the first Ad Council campaigns was during World War II, using the slogan "Loose Lips Sink Ships."

—Adapted from Goldsmith, *Consumer Economics: Issues and Behaviors*, 2nd ed., p. 215.

_____ 6. Sentences 1 and 2 are _____.
   a. main ideas
   b. major supporting details
   c. minor supporting details

_____ 7. Sentence 4 is a _____.
   a. main idea
   b. major supporting detail
   c. minor supporting detail

_____ 8. Sentence 5 is a _____.
   a. main idea
   b. major supporting detail
   c. minor supporting detail

_____ 9. Sentence 6 is a _____.
   a. main idea
   b. major supporting detail
   c. minor supporting detail

_____ 10. Sentence 7 is a _____.
   a. main idea
   b. major supporting detail
   c. minor supporting detail

Chapter 7: Supporting Details, Outlines, and Concept Maps
LAB 7.5 MASTERY TEST 1

Name _____ Section _____ Date _____ Score (number correct) _____ x 10 = _____

Directions: Read each paragraph and answer the questions that follow.

[1]The Great Depression caused widespread hardships. [2]One hardship was lack of food and public aid. [3]For example, in the spring of 1932, thousands of Americans faced starvation. [4]In Philadelphia, relief funds could not be accessed for 11 days. [5]As a result, hundreds of families lived on stale bread, thin soup, and garbage. [6]Given the nation as a whole, only about one-fourth of the jobless received any public aid. [7]Another problem was housing. [8]In Birmingham, Alabama, landlords in poor areas gave up trying to collect rents. [9]They preferred, as one Alabama congressman told a Senate committee, "to have somebody living there free of charge rather than to have the house. . .burned up for fuel [by scavengers]." [10]Many people were evicted from their homes. [11]They often gathered in rickety communities made of packing boxes, rusty sheet metal, and similar refuse they built on swamps, garbage dumps, and other wasteland. [12]People began to call these places "Hoovervilles." [13]Thousands of tramps roamed the countryside begging and hunting for food.

—Adapted from Garraty and Carnes, *The American Nation: A History of the United States*, 10th ed., p. 712.

_____ 1. Sentence 1 is a
    a. main idea.
    b. major supporting detail.
    c. minor supporting detail.

_____ 2. Sentence 2 is a
    a. main idea.
    b. major supporting detail.
    c. minor supporting detail.

_____ 3. Sentence 3 is a
    a. main idea.
    b. major supporting detail.
    c. minor supporting detail.

_____ 4. Sentence 5 is a
    a. main idea.
    b. major supporting detail.
    c. minor supporting detail.

_____ 5. Sentence 7 is a
    a. main idea.
    b. major supporting detail.
    c. minor supporting detail.

Writing Business Letters

[1]Good business letters follow some standard practices and well-known formats and guidelines. [2]Most business letters are presented in either block format or modified block format. [3]The **modified block format** is often used for longer letters. [4]In this format, the return address and the closing and signature are centered on the page. [5]But the paragraphs are not indented from the left margin. [6]The **block format** is often used for short letters. [7]In this format, all paragraphs are flush at the left margin. [8]This includes the greeting and the signature. [9]In both styles, notations following the signature are flush left. [10]This includes initials for the writer and typist (RL:gw), *Enc.* or *Enclosure,* or *cc: Nancy Harris* (the name of a person sent a copy).

—Adapted from Anson and Schwegler, *The Longman Handbook for Writers and Readers,* Copyright © 1997 pp. 52–53.

_____ 6. Sentence 1 is a
    a. central idea.   c. major supporting detail.
    b. main idea.   d. minor supporting detail.

_____ 7. Sentence 2 is a
    a. central idea.   c. major supporting detail.
    b. main idea.   d. minor supporting detail.

_____ 8. Sentence 3 is a
    a. central idea.   c. major supporting detail.
    b. main idea.   d. minor supporting detail.

_____ 9. Sentence 6 is a
    a. central idea.   c. major supporting detail.
    b. main idea.   d. minor supporting detail.

_____ 10. Sentence 10 is a
    a. central idea.   c. major supporting detail.
    b. main idea.   d. minor supporting detail.

Name _____ Section_____ Date_____Score (number correct) _____ x 10 = _____

Directions: Read the following paragraphs and answer the questions that follow.

[1]Chemicals that cause harm to the unborn are called teratogens. [2]One teratogen that affects the development of human embryos in the womb causes birth defects. [3]An example involves the drug thalidomide, developed in the 1950s as a sleeping pill and to prevent nausea during pregnancy. [4]Tragically, the drug turned out to be a powerful teratogen, and its use caused birth defects in thousands of babies. [5]Even a single dose during pregnancy could result in limb deformities and organ defects. [6]Thalidomide was banned in the 1960s once scientists recognized its connection with birth defects. [7]Ironically, today the drug shows promise in treating a wide range of diseases, including Alzheimer's disease, AIDS, and various types of cancer.

—Withgott and Brennan, *Environment: The Science Behind the Stories*, 3rd ed., p. 390.

_____ 1. Sentence 1 is a
   a. main idea.
   b. major supporting detail.
   c. minor supporting detail.

_____ 2. Sentence 2 is a
   a. main idea.
   b. major supporting detail.
   c. minor supporting detail.

_____ 3. Sentence 3 is a
   a. main idea.
   b. major supporting detail.
   c. minor supporting detail.

[1]Both the quality and quantity of sleep are affected by a number of factors. [2]Illness that causes pain or physical distress is one major problem that can result in sleep problems. [3]People who are ill require more sleep than normal, and the normal rhythm of sleep and wakefulness is often disturbed. [4]People deprived of REM sleep subsequently spend more sleep time than normal in this stage. [5]Respiratory conditions can also disturb an individual's sleep. [6]Shortness of breath often makes sleep difficult, and people who have nasal congestion or sinus drainage may have trouble breathing and hence may find it difficult to sleep. [7]Certain endocrine disturbances are another cause of sleeping problems. [8]Hyperthyroidism lengthens pre-sleep time, making it difficult for a client to fall asleep. [9]Hypothyroidism, conversely, decreases stage IV sleep. [10]Women with low levels of estrogen often report excessive fatigue. [11]In addition, they may experience sleep disruptions due, in part, to the discomfort associated with hot flashes or night sweats that can occur with reduced estrogen levels.

—Adapted from Berman et al., Kozier and Erb's *Fundamentals of Nursing: Concepts, Process, and Practice,* 8th ed., pp. 1169–1170.

_____ 4. Sentence 1 is a
   a. main idea.
   b. major supporting detail.
   c. minor supporting detail.

_____ 5 Sentence 2 is a
   a. main idea.
   b. major supporting detail.
   c. minor supporting detail.

_____ 6. Sentence 3 is a
   a. main idea.
   b. major supporting detail.
   c. minor supporting detail.

_____ 7. Sentence 5 is a
   a. main idea.
   b. major supporting detail.
   c. minor supporting detail.

_____ 8. Sentence 6 is a
   a. main idea.
   b. major supporting detail.
   c. minor supporting detail.

_____ 9. Sentence 7 is a
   a. main idea.
   b. major supporting detail.
   c. minor supporting detail.

_____ 10. Sentence 11 is a
   a. main idea.
   b. major supporting detail.
   c. minor supporting detail.

Chapter 8: Outlines and Concept Maps
LAB 8.1 PRACTICE EXERCISE 1

Name _____ Section _____ Date _____ Score (number correct) _____ x 10 = _____

Objective: To create an outline by using the major and minor details.

Directions: Read the passage and answer the questions that follow.

A. [1]If you have trouble getting a good night's sleep, the following three tips may help. [2]First, people who exercise sleep better. [3]Most who exercise for 30 minutes four times a week fall asleep faster and sleep longer. [4]Exercise at least two hours before bedtime to give your body time to relax after exercising. [5]Second, certain foods affect sleep. [6]Avoid caffeine and nicotine; both are stimulants. [7]On the other hand, bananas, cottage cheese, turkey, tuna, and calcium help the body create sleep hormones. [8]Finally, calming habits lead to peaceful sleep. [9]Use relaxation techniques. [10]For example, breathe deeply, and tighten and relax each muscle. [11]Take a warm bath, and go to bed at the same time every night.

_____1. The topic of this paragraph is _____.
  a. exercising
  b. sleeping
  c. healthy eating
  d. relaxing

_____2. In general, the major details of this passage are _____.
  a. a list of suggestions for better sleep
  b. reasons why people have difficulty sleeping
  c. examples of exercise regimens
  d. an explanation of relaxation techniques

_____3. What phrase in the stated main idea indicates the major details?
  a. if you have trouble
  b. getting a good night's sleep
  c. following three tips
  d. may help

_____4. What signal word introduces the last major detail?
  a. if
  b. second
  c. on the other hand
  d. finally

_____5. Sentence 10 is a(n) _____.
  a. main idea sentence
  b. major supporting detail
  c. minor supporting detail
  d. irrelevant fact

B. [1]An examination of vulnerable populations in U.S. society begins with considering issues in social work practice related to women. [2]Although women make up more than one-half of the population, they do not share the same advantages as their male counterparts. [3]First of all, women are not compensated equally for their work. [4]For example, the median income for married couples with children under 18 was $63,110; for single mothers with children under 18, it was $24,693. [5]Another disadvantage is that women are more vulnerable. [6]For instance, violence is a major issue with approximately 1.5 million women being raped or assaulted each year by an intimate partner. [7]A third disadvantage concerns their status within the family. [8]For example, men who have higher education and employment than women often use this fact as justification for their exerting power and control over wives and children. [9]Correspondingly, women typically have primary responsibility for the unpaid work of childrearing, caretaking, and maintaining the household, thus ensuring their subordinate status with in the family.

—Adapted from Morales, Sheafor, and Scott, *Social Work: A Profession of Many Faces*,
12th ed., p. 255.

_____ 6. Sentence 2 serves as a _____ for the paragraph.
   a. topic
   b. main idea
   c. major detail supporting the main idea
   d. minor detail supporting a major detail

_____ 7. Sentence 3 serves as a _____ for the paragraph.
   a. topic
   b. main idea
   c. major detail supporting the main idea
   d. minor detail supporting a major detail

_____ 8. Sentence 4 serves as a _____ for the paragraph.
   a. topic
   b. main idea
   c. major detail supporting the main idea
   d. minor detail supporting a major detail

9-10. Fill in the outline by completing the heading and filling in the major detail that is missing.

_____(9) shared by women

   1. Lower compensation for work
   2. More vulnerable to harm
   3. _____(10)

Chapter 8: Outlines and Concept Maps
LAB 8.2 PRACTICE EXERCISE 2

Name _____ Section_____ Date_____Score (number correct) _____ x 10 = _____

Objective: To use the table of contents to understand the relationship between general and specific ideas.

A. Directions: Read the partial table of contents from a college health textbook and answer the questions that follow.

Chapter 1   Promoting Health Behavior

—Donatelle, *Health: The Basics,* 4th ed., p. iii.

_____ 1. How many chapters are listed?
    a. three   c. five
    b. four   d. eight

_____ 2. Which part includes chapters on addictions?
    a. Part I
    b. Part II
    c. Part III
    d. Chapter 4

_____ 3. How many chapters are devoted to creating a balanced lifestyle?
    a. one   c. three
    b. two   d. five

_____ 4. Which chapter discusses the importance of making commitments in personal relationships?
    a. Chapter 2   c. Chapter 5
    b. Chapter 3   d. Chapter 8

_____ 5. In which chapter does the author discuss managing stress?
   a. Chapter 2   c. Chapter 4
   b. Chapter 3   d. Chapter 5

B. Directions: Read the remainder of the table of contents from the college health textbook and answer the questions that follow.

_____ 6. How many major sections are in the book?
   a. 3   c. 6
   b. 4   d. 16

_____ 7. In which chapter would you expect to read about the importance of physical fitness?
   a. 9   c. 11
   b. 10   d. 16

_____ 8. In which section would you expect to read about steps in first aid?
   a. Part V   c. Appendix B
   b. Appendix A   d. Chapter 12

_____ 9. How many chapters are devoted to the topic of disease?
   a. 2   c. 5
   b. 4   d. 7

_____ 10. In which chapter would you expect to read about pesticides?
   a. Chapter 13   c. Chapter 15
   b. Chapter 14   d. Chapter 16

Name _____ Section _____ Date _____ Score (number correct) _____ x 10 = _____

Directions: Read the following paragraph and answer the questions that follow.

A. Self-talk, which includes three cognitive procedures, is the way you think and talk to yourself, and it can play a role in modifying your health-related behaviors. One procedure is rational-emotional therapy, which is based on the premise that there is a close connection between what people say to themselves and how they feel. According to psychologist Albert Ellis, most everyday emotional problems and related behaviors stem from irrational statements that people make to themselves when events in their lives are different from what they would like them to be. Another procedure is Meichenbaum's self-instructional methods. In these therapies, clients are encouraged to give "self-instructions" ("Slow down, don't rush") and "positive affirmations" ("My speech is going fine—I'm almost done!") to themselves instead of thinking self-defeating thoughts ("I'm talking too fast—my speech is terrible.") whenever a situation seems out of control. The final procedure is called blocking/thought stopping. By purposefully blocking or stopping negative thoughts, a person can concentrate on taking positive steps toward necessary behavior change. For example, suppose you are preoccupied with your ex-partner, who has recently deserted you for someone else. In blocking/thought stopping, you consciously stop thinking about the situation and force yourself to think about something more pleasant (e.g., dinner tomorrow with your best friend).

—Adapted from Donatelle, *Health: The Basics,* 4th ed. pp. 20–21.

_____ 1. The topic of this paragraph is
  a. psychology.
  b. cognitive psychology.
  c. Meichenbaum's self-instructional methods.
  d. self-talk.

_____ 2. In general, the major details of this passage are
  a. the reasons we suffer from bad health.
  b. procedures which can modify behavior.
  c. a study about how to modify behavior.
  d. examples of positive behavior.

_____ 3. What signal word in the stated main idea indicates the number of major details?
  a. three   c. role
  b. cognitive   d. behaviors

_____ 4. What signal word introduces the third major detail?
  a. another   c. whenever
  b. first   d. final

_____ 5. The sentence that includes ("My speech is going fine—I'm almost done!") is a(n)
   a. main idea sentence.
   b. major supporting detail.
   c. minor supporting detail.
   d. irrelevant fact.

B. Directions: Read the following passage and answer the questions that follow.

The Modern Bureaucracy

In 1831, describing President Andrew Jackson's populating the federal government with his political cronies, Senator William Learned Marcy of New York commented, "To the victor belong the spoils." From his statement derives the phrase **spoils system** to describe the firing of public officeholders of the defeated political party and their replacement with loyalists of the new administration. Many presidents, including Jackson, argued that in order to implement their policies, they had to be able to appoint those who subscribed to their political views as rewards for their support.

Increasing public criticism of the spoils system prompted Congress to pass the Civil Service Reform Act, more commonly known as the **Pendleton Act,** in 1883 to reduce patronage. It established the principle of federal employment on the basis of open, competitive exams and created the bipartisan three-member Civil Service Commission, which operated until 1978. Initially, only about 10 percent of the positions in the federal **civil service system** were covered, but later laws and executive orders have extended coverage of the act to over 90 percent of all federal employees. This new system was called the **merit system,** and it classified civil service jobs into grades or levels.

The civil service system as it has evolved today provides a powerful base for federal agencies and bureaucrats. Federal workers have tenure, and the leverage of politicians is reduced. The good part is that the spoils system was reduced (but not eliminated). The bad part, however, is that federal agencies can and often do take on a life of their own, making administrative law, passing judgments, and so on. With 90 percent of federal workers secure in their positions, some bureaucrats have been able to thwart reforms passed by legislators and wanted by the people. This often makes the bureaucracy the target of public criticism and citizen frustration.

—Adapted from O'Connor and Sabato, *The Essentials of American Government,*
Copyright © 1998, p. 217.

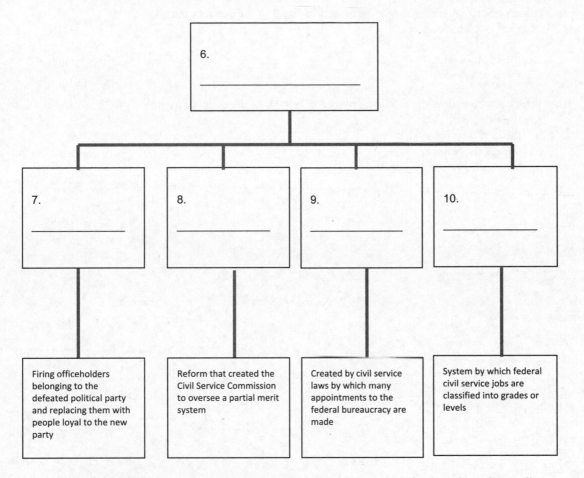

_____ 6. Which of the following should be placed in box 6 to accurately show how the reading passage is organized?
   a. the Pendleton Act
   b. the civil service system
   c. The current U.S. civil service system has evolved over the years.
   d. the spoils system

_____ 7. Which of the following should be placed in box 7 of the concept map?
   a. the Pendleton Act
   b. the civil service system
   c. The current U.S. civil service system has evolved over the years.
   d. the spoils system

_____ 8. Which of the following should be placed in box 8 of the concept map?
   a. the Pendleton Act
   b. the civil service system
   c. The current U.S. civil service system has evolved over the years.
   d. the spoils system

113

____ 9. Which of the following should be placed in box 9 of the concept map?
   a. the Pendleton Act
   b. the civil service system
   c. the spoils system
   d. the merit system

____ 10. Which of the following should be placed in box 10 of the concept map?
   a. the Pendleton Act
   b. the civil service system
   c. the spoils system
   d. the merit system

Name _____ Section_____ Date_____Score (number correct) _____ x 10 = _____

Directions: Read the passage and answer the questions that follow.

¹How much do you know about personal finance? ²Being financially secure involves more than just making money. ³Financial planning is an ongoing process that involves five basic steps no matter what your circumstances.

⁴Financial planning begins with an examination of your current financial situation. ⁵Determine how much money you make. ⁶Keep track of what you spend by taking a few minutes each day to enter all of the day's expenses into a book or computer program.

⁷The second step of the financial planning process is defining your goals. ⁸Write them down. ⁹Attach costs to them. ¹⁰Determine when the money to accomplish those goals will be needed.

¹¹The third step of the process is developing an action plan to achieve your goals. ¹²A solid personal financial plan includes an informed and controlled budget, determines your investment strategy, and reflects your unique personal goals.

¹³Next, implement your plan. ¹⁴Although it's important to develop a financial plan, it is equally important to actually stick to that plan. ¹⁵Keep in mind that your financial plan is not the goal; it is the tool you use to achieve your goals.

¹⁶Finally, review your progress. ¹⁷You may have to reevaluate your strategies as time passes and circumstances change. ¹⁸Be prepared to revise your plan.

—Adapted from Keown, *Personal Finance: Turning Money into Wealth*, 5th ed., pp. 5–6.

_____1. The topic this passage is _____.
   a. the financial planning process
   b. ways to build up savings
   c. planning for the unexpected
   d. financial record keeping

_____2. The central idea is stated in _____.
   a. sentence 1
   b. sentence 2
   c. sentence 3
   d. sentence 4

_____3. The central idea of the passage is supported by _____.
   a. examples of financial plans
   b. statistics that demonstrate the effectiveness of financial planning
   c. testimony by financial planners
   d. basic steps of personal financial planning

_____4. Sentences 4, 7, 11, 13, and 16 serve as _____.
   a. central themes
   b. main ideas
   c. major supporting details
   d. minor supporting details

_____5. Sentences 8, 9, and 10 serve as _____ for the paragraph.
   a. central themes
   b. main ideas
   c. major supporting details
   d. minor supporting details

6-10. Fill in the outline by completing the major and minor details that are missing.

The Personal Financial Planning Process

1. (6)_____
   a. Determine income
   b. Record expenses

2. Define your goals
   a. (7)_____
   b. Attach costs
   c. Develop a timeline

3. (8)_____
   a. Include a budget
   b. Include an investment strategy
   c. Reflect personal goals

4. (9)_____

5. Review your progress
   a. (10)_____
   b. Revise your plan

Name _____ Section_____ Date_____Score (number correct) _____ x 10 = _____

Directions: Read the passages and answer the questions that follow.

A. Do you have to be happy all of the time to achieve overall subjective well-being? Of course not. Everyone experiences disappointments, unhappiness, and times when life seems unfair. However, people with an overall sense of subjective well-being are typically resilient, are able to look on the positive side, get themselves back on track fairly quickly, and are less likely to fall into deep despair over setbacks. There are several myths about happiness: that it depends on age, gender, race, and socioeconomic status. Research and empirical evidence, however, have debunked these four myths:

- *There is no "happiest age."* Age is not a predictor of subjective well-being. Most age groups exhibit similar levels of life satisfaction, although the things that bring joy often change with age.
- *Happiness has no "gender gap."* Women are more likely than men to suffer from anxiety and depression, and men are more at risk for alcoholism and personality disorders. Equal numbers of men and women report being fairly satisfied with life.
- *There are minimal racial differences in happiness.* For example, African Americans and European Americans report nearly the same levels of happiness, and African Americans are slightly less vulnerable to depression. Despite racism and discrimination, members of disadvantaged minority groups generally seem to "think optimistically" by making realistic self-comparisons and attributing problems less to themselves than to unfair circumstances.
- *Money does not buy happiness.* Wealthier societies report greater well-being. However, once the basic necessities of food, shelter, and safety are provided, there is a very weak correlation between income and happiness. Having no money is a cause of misery, but wealth itself does not guarantee happiness.

Fortunately, humans are remarkably resourceful creatures. We respond to great loss, such as the death of a loved one or a traumatic event, with an initial period of grief, mourning, and sometimes abject rage. Yet, with time and the support of loving family and friends, we can pick ourselves up, brush off the bad times, and manage to find satisfaction and peace. Typically, humans learn from suffering and emerge even stronger and more ready to deal with the next crisis.

—Adapted from Donatelle, *Health: The Basics*, 6th ed., p. 41.

_____ 1.   In general, the major details of this passage are
    a.   reasons we have myths.
    b.   characteristics of good health.
    c.   examples of healthy habits.
    d.   myths about happiness.

_____ 2.   One of the traits of subjective well-being is
    a.   resilience.
    b.   a pessimistic view of life.
    c.   difficulty in bouncing back from disappointments.
    d.   falling into deep despair over setbacks.

_____ 3. How many major details are mentioned in this passage?

     a. one   c. three

     b. two   d. four

_____ 4. The sentence "For example, African Americans and European Americans report nearly the same levels of happiness, and African-Americans are slightly less vulnerable to depression." is a

     a. main idea sentence.

     b. major supporting detail.

     c. minor supporting detail.

     d. concluding sentence.

_____ 5. According to the passage, happiness

     a. depends on age.

     b. is experienced more by women than by men.

     c. has a weak correlation to income.

     d. is more directly related to ethnic group.

B. A segmented body resembling a series of fused rings is the hallmark of phylum Annelida (from the Latin *anellus*, ring). (…) Annelids range in length from less than 1 mm to 3 m, the length of some giant Australian earthworms. They are found in damp soil, in the sea, and in most freshwater habitats. Some aquatic annelids swim in pursuit of food, but most are bottom-dwelling scavengers that burrow in sand and mud. There are three main groups of annelids: earthworms, and their relatives, polychaetes, and leeches.

Earthworms and Their Relatives. Figure 18.10A illustrates the segmented anatomy of an earthworm. Internally, the coelom is partitioned by membrane walls (only a few are fully shown here). Many of the internal body structures are repeated within each segment. The nervous system (yellow) includes a simple brain and a ventral nerve cord with a cluster of nerve cells in each segment. (…)

Polychaetes. The polychaetes (from the Greek *polys*, many, and *chaeta*, hair) form the largest group of annelids. (…) Each segment of a polychaete has a pair of fleshy, paddle-like appendages with many stiff bristles (called chaetae) that help the worm wriggle about in search of small invertebrates to eat. In many polychaetes, the appendages are richly supplied with blood vessels and function in gas exchange. (…).

Leeches. The third main group of annelids is the leeches, which are notorious for their bloodsucking habits. However, most species are free-living carnivores that eat small invertebrates such as snails and insects. The majority of leeches inhabit fresh water, but there are also marine species and a few terrestrial species that inhabit moist vegetation in the tropics. They range in length from 1 to 30 cm.

—Adapted from Campbell, Reece, Taylor, and Simon, *Biology: Concepts and Connections*, 5th ed., pp. 378–379.

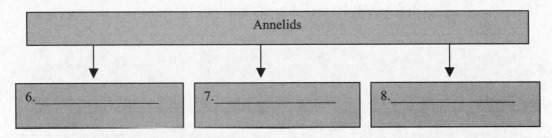

6–8. Fill in the blanks of the concept map with the main idea and major details from the passage.

_____ 9. Which word or phrase signals the number of boxes to include in the concept map?
     a. series of fused rings   c. each
     b. three main groups   d. also

_____ 10. Which word signals the third major point?
     a. three   c. illustrates
     b. largest   d. third

119

Name _____ Section _____ Date _____ Score (number correct) _____ x 10 = _____

Directions: Read the following passages and answer the questions that follow.

Modeling, or learning behaviors through careful observation of other people, is one of the most effective strategies for changing behavior. Suppose that you have great difficulty talking to people you don't know very well. Effective communication is essential to achieving optimum health. One of the easiest ways to improve your communication skills is to select friends whose "gift of gab" you envy. Observe their social skills. What do they say? How do they act? Do they talk more or listen more? How do people respond to them? Why are they such good communicators? Another example is to observe people who are successful in the career to which you aspire. Consider their strategies to work their way up the ladder. What courses did they study in college? What kind of internship did they land? What advantages did they make for themselves that you could pursue? By carefully observing the behaviors of the people you admire and isolating their components, you can model the steps of your behavior change strategy on a proven success.

—Adapted from Donatelle, *Health: The Basics,* 4th ed., p. 20.

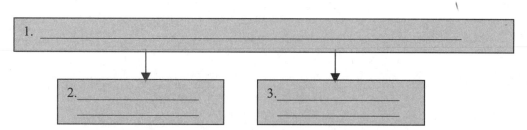

_____ 1. Choose the correct item for the first blank in the concept map.
   a. Modeling is one of the most effective strategies for changing behavior.
   b. Effective communication is essential to achieving optimum health.
   c. One of the easiest ways to improve your communication skills is to select friends whose "gift of gab" you envy.
   d. By carefully observing the behaviors of the people you admire and isolating their components, you can model the steps of your behavior change strategy on a proven success.

_____ 2. Choose the correct item for the second blank in the concept map.
   a. Suppose that you have great difficulty talking to people you don't know very well.
   b. Effective communication is essential to achieving optimum health.
   c. One of the easiest ways to improve your communication skills is to select friends whose "gift of gab" you envy.
   d. Observe their social skills.

_____ 3. Choose the correct item for the third blank in the concept map.
   a. Another example is to observe people who are successful in the career to which you aspire.
   b. Consider their strategies to work their way up the ladder.
   c. What courses did they study in college?
   d. What advantages did they make for themselves that you could pursue?

_____ 4. Which word signals the first major supporting detail?
   a. suppose   c. essential
   b. effective   d. one

_____ 5. Which word(s) signal the second major supporting detail?
   a. why   c. what
   b. another example d. by

B. Although schooling is vital for all children, educating girls has an especially powerful impact on the welfare of families, societies, and future generations. The diverse benefits of girls' schooling largely accrue in several ways. The first way is through enhanced verbal skills—reading, writing, and oral communication. In studies carried out on three continents, in three cultures, and in three community settings—rural Nepal, a small Mexican town, and a large city in Zambia—the more education women obtained, the better their language and literacy skills. Girls were helping their parents read instructions on prescription medicines, making better choices while shopping, and explaining the news on television. The second benefit occurs through a sense of empowerment. The girls in these studies developed higher aspirations and envisioned a better life for themselves. Instead of laboring in the fields and being confined to their homes, these girls now saw themselves becoming teachers or doctors. Finally, the third benefit is seen in better family relationships and parenting. The empowerment that springs from education is associated with more equitable husband-wife relationships and a reduction in harsh disciplining of children. Educated mothers engage in more verbal stimulation and teaching of literacy skills to their children, which fosters success in school, higher educational attainment, and economic gains in the next generation. According to a recent United Nations report, the education of girls is the most effective means of combating the most profound global threats to human development: poverty, maternal and child mortality, and disease.

—Adapted from Berk, *Development Through the Lifespan*, 4th ed., p. 62.

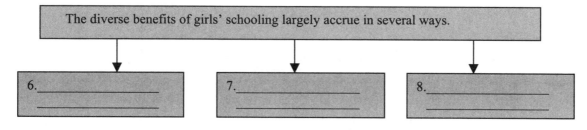

The diverse benefits of girls' schooling largely accrue in several ways.

6. _____
_____

7. _____
_____

8. _____
_____

6–8. Fill in the blanks of the concept map with the major details from the passage.

_____ 9. Which word(s) signal the first major supporting detail?
    a. although   c. in studies
    b. the first way   d. three cultures

_____ 10. Which word(s) signal the last major supporting detail?
    a. the second benefit   c. finally
    b. instead of   d. according to

Chapter 9: Transitions and Thought Patterns
LAB 9.1 PRACTICE EXERCISE 1

Name _____ Section _____ Date _____ Score (number correct) _____ x 10 = _____

Objective: To identify the correct transitions and the relationship of ideas between sentences.

Directions: Read each set of sentences and answer the questions that follow them.

A. It is best to avoid arguing _____ you are angry.

_____1. Which transition best completes the sentence?
    a. until
    b. when
    c. and
    d. during

_____2. What type of transition is used in this sentence?
    a. time order
    b. addition
    c. space order
    d. classification

B. Most states use a system to assign new prisoners to initial prisons based on the type of their offense, perceived dangerousness, and escape risk. A prisoner might be assigned to a _____ of minimum-, medium-, or maximum-custody institution.

—Adapted from Schmalleger, *Criminal Justice: A Brief Introduction*, 8th ed., p. 400.

_____3. Which transition best completes the sentence?
    a. finally
    b. over
    c. furthermore
    d. category

_____4. The relationship of the ideas between the two sentences is one of _____?
    a. time order
    b. addition
    c. space order
    d. classification

Directions: Fill in each blank with the correct transition word from the words in the box. Use each word only once.

A) first	C) third	E) as
B) second	D) and	F) when

Focus: A Foundation for Success

A foundation for any kind of success is the ability to focus. **(5)** _____, focusing enables us to solve problems. For example, some people are terrible at spelling, **(6)** _____ paying close attention or focusing on how words look when they are correctly spelled improves spelling. **(7)** _____, focusing produces better work. For instance, many of us have sloppy handwriting, yet **(8)** _____ we slow down and concentrate, we can control the way we form our letters. **(9)** _____, focusing keeps us from becoming distracted. **(10)** _____ we seriously focus on the teacher's instruction, we do not allow a classmate to turn our attention away.

5. _____

6. _____

7. _____

8. _____

9. _____

10. _____

Chapter 9: Transitions and Thought Patterns
LAB 9.2 PRACTICE EXERCISE 2

Name _____ Section _____ Date _____ Score (number correct) _____ x 10 = _____

Objective: To identify the pattern of thought and to choose transitions that best show the relationship among sentences in a paragraph.

A. Directions: Identify the thought pattern indicated by each of the following sentences taken from a college government textbook.

_____ 1. There are two basic types of lobbyists.
    a. time order   c. listing
    b. space order   d. classification

_____ 2. Long ago, the Speaker was king of the congressional mountain.
    a. time order   c. listing
    b. space order   d. classification

_____ 3. Another activity unique to the Senate is the filibuster.
    a. time order   c. listing
    b. space order   d. classification

_____ 4. At the center is big business.
    a. time order   c. listing
    b. space order   d. classification

B. Directions: Read the following passage from a psychology textbook and fill in the blanks with the letter that indicates the correct transition word from the box. Use each word once.

A) later	**C)** as	**E)** begin
B) next	**D)** finally	**F)** then

[1]To explain the emotional and social development in infancy and toddlerhood, we ___5___ with Erikson's psychosocial theory, which provides an overview of personality development during infancy and toddlerhood. [2]___6___ we chart the course of emotional development. [3]___7___ we do so, we will discover why fear and anger become more apparent by the end of a baby's first year. [4]Our attention ___8___ turns to individual differences in temperament. [5]We will examine biological and environmental contributions to these differences and their consequences for future development. [6]___9___, we take up attachment to the caregiver, the child's first affectionate tie. [7]We will see how the feelings of security that grow out

of this important bond provide support for the child's sense of independence and expanding social relationships. [8]___10____, we focus on early self-development. [9]By the end of toddlerhood, children recognize themselves in mirrors and photographs and show the beginnings of self-control. [10]Cognitive advances combine with social experiences to produce these changes during the second year.

—Adapted from Berk, *Development Through the Lifespan,* 4th ed., pp. 183–184.

5. The best transition for the blank in sentence 1 is _____.

6. The best transition for the blank in sentence 2 is _____.

7. The best transition for the blank in sentence 3 is _____.

8. The best transition for the first blank in sentence 4 is _____.

9. The best transition for the second blank in sentence 6 is _____.

10. The best transition for the blank in sentence 8 is _____.

Chapter 9: Transitions and Thought Patterns
LAB 9.REVIEW TEST 1

Name _____ Section _____ Date _____ Score (number correct) _____ x 10 = _____

Directions: Identify the correct transition word; then identify the type of transition you chose.

A. Kristina slept for two days_____ driving from Florida to Wisconsin without stopping.

_____ 1. The best transition word for the sentence is
   a. after.   c. while.
   b. and.   d. during.

_____ 2. The relationship between the ideas is one of
   a. time order.   c. listing.
   b. space order.   d. classification.

B. Many college students like to gamble because they want to make extra money, _____ they enjoy the risk and excitement.

_____ 3. The best transition word for the sentence is
   a. next.   c. after.
   b. and.   d. while.

_____ 4. The relationship between the ideas is one of
   a. space.   c. time order.
   b. classification.   d. addition.

C. Successful businesses focus on short-term and long-term goals. _____, they set long-term goals; then those goals shape the short-term goals.

_____ 5. The best transition word for the sentence is _____.
   a. First   c. Next
   b. Finally   d. Moreover

Directions: Read the paragraph and answer the questions that follow.

[1]Traditional democratic theory holds that ordinary citizens have the good sense to reach political judgments and that government has the capacity to act on those judgments. [2]Today, however, we live in a society of experts whose technical knowledge overshadows the knowledge of the general population. [3]What, after all, does the average citizen—however conscientious—know about eligibility criteria for welfare, agricultural price supports, foreign competition, and the hundreds of other issues that confront government each year? [4]Years ago, the power of the few—the elite—might have been based on property holdings. [5]_____, the elite are likely to be those who command knowledge, the experts. [6]Even the most rigorous democratic theory does not demand that citizens be experts on everything, but as human knowledge has expanded, it has become

127

increasingly difficult for individual citizens to make well-informed decisions. ⁷Because citizens today do not seem to take their citizenship seriously, democracy's defenders worry. ⁸Furthermore, they worry that now Americans do not take full advantage of their opportunities to shape government or select its leaders.

—Adapted from Edwards, Wattenberg, and Lineberry,
Government in America: People, Politics, and Policy, 12th ed., p. 18.

_____ 6. What thought pattern is suggested by the word "today" in sentence 2?
a. time order
b. space order
c. listing
d. classification

_____ 7. "Years ago" in sentence 4 shows
a. time order.
b. space order.
c. listing.
d. classification.

_____ 8. The best transition word for the blank in sentence 5 is
a. since.
b. later.
c. now.
d. final.

_____ 9. What relationship is suggested by the word "furthermore" in sentence 7?
a. time order
b. space order
c. listing
d. classification

_____ 10. The thought pattern for this paragraph is
a. time order.
b. space order.
c. listing.
d. classification.

Chapter 9: Transitions and Thought Patterns
LAB 9.4 REVIEW TEST 2

Name _____ Section _____ Date _____ Score (number correct) _____ x 10 = _____

Directions: Read each set of sentences and answer the questions that follow them.

A. Muffy, a two-year-old Yorkshire terrier, loved going for rides in the car _____ one car ride took her to the veterinarian's office.

_____1. Which transition best completes the sentence?
    a. until
    b. when
    c. and
    d. during

_____2. What type of transition is used in this sentence?
    a. time order
    b. addition
    c. space order
    d. classification

B. Children who attend Head Start programs gain a boost in IQ scores that lasts for a few years, _____more of these children graduate from high school than children who do not attend such a program.

_____3. Which transition best completes the sentence?
    a. until
    b. once
    c. moreover
    d. during

_____4. What type of transition is used in this sentence?
    a. time order
    b. addition
    c. space order
    d. classification

Directions: Fill in each blank with the correct transition word from the words in the box. Use each word only once.

A) second	C) for one thing	E) also
B) In addition	D) finally	F) many

A **brand** is a name, term, sign, symbol, or design, or combination of these, that identifies the maker or seller of a product or service. Branding helps buyers and sellers in (5) _____ ways. (6)_____, brand names help consumers identify products that might benefit them. (7)_____ brands (8)_____ say something about product quality and consistency—buyers who always buy the same brand know that they will get the same features, benefits, and quality each time they buy. (9) _____, branding also gives the seller several advantages. The brand name becomes the basis on which a whole story can be built about a product's special qualities. (10)_____, branding helps the seller to segment markets. For example, Toyota Motor Corporation can offer the major Lexus, Toyota, and Scion brands, each with numerous sub-brands—such as Camry, Prius, Matrix, and others—not just one general product for all consumers.

—Adapted from Kotler and Armstrong, *Principles of Marketing*, 13th ed., p. 231.

Name _____ Section _____ Date _____ Score (number correct) _____ x 10 = _____

Directions: Choose the best transition word for each sentence.

Maxine bought a new car and _____ gave her old car to her needy brother.

____ 1. The best transition word for the sentence is
    a. another.   c. then.
    b. and.   d. first

____ 2. The relationship between the ideas is one of
    a. addition.   c. classification.
    b. time order.   d. space order.

Sometimes John can be hurtfully rude; _____ he had made plans with his girlfriend's family for dinner, he ran into an old friend and missed the dinner.

____ 3. Which transition best completes the sentence?
    a. after   c. finally
    b. in addition   d. and

____ 4. The relationship between the ideas is one of
    a. time order.   c. classification.
    b. addition.   d. space order

Directions: Read the paragraph and answer the questions that follow.

[1] While preparing a speech, you must decide the order in which to present the main points. [2] Mind-mapping is one strategy where you visually "map out" how the various ideas connect. [3] In a mind-map, one starts in the center with a word or symbol, and then writes down all the things that come to mind about that word or topic. [4] If you were mind-mapping a speech about fine arts, you might begin with a circle labeled "the fine arts" and then identify all the aspects of the fine arts that should be considered around that circle. [5] Another strategy identified is the narrative or storytelling. [6] A story in a speech doesn't have to be long and involved and need not follow the gridlines for traditional stories. [7] A _____ pattern is the time-sequence pattern or chronological pattern. [8] The key to this is to follow a natural time sequence and avoid jumping haphazardly from one date to another. 9 These are just three of the eight types of patterns you can choose for your speech.

—Adapted from Seiler and Beall, *Communication: Making Connections*, 7th ed., pp. 220–222.

_____ 6. The word "center" in sentence 3 indicates
   a. time order.   c. listing.
   b. space order.   d. classification.

_____ 7. The transition "begin" in sentence 4 shows
   a. time order.   c. listing.
   b. space order.   d. classification.

_____ 8. What relationship is suggested by the word "another" in sentence 5?
   a. time order.   c. listing.
   b. space order.   d. classification.

_____ 9. The best transition word for the blank in sentence 7 is
   a. since.   c. beginning.
   b. later.   d. third.

_____ 10. The thought pattern for this paragraph is
   a. time order.   c. listing.
   b. space order.   d. classification.

Name _____ Section _____ Date _____ Score (number correct) _____ x 10 = _____

Directions: Read the following passages from a psychology textbook and fill in the blanks with the best transition.

[1]If you are a parent, you have almost certainly considered the question, "To spank or not to spank?" [2]Spanking is quite common—but what are the consequences for children who are often spanked? [3]Why is this a difficult question to answer? [4]First, no researchers could ethically conduct an experiment in which they expose children to physical punishment. [5]Researchers, instead, try to assess whether a relationship exists between the amount of physical punishment children have experienced and negative aspects of their behavior. [6]This leads to _____ problem with research on spanking. [7]Parents may be unwilling or unable to give accurate indications of how _____ they spanked their children. [8]A _____ problem is getting accurate data on the child behaviors that led parents to spank them. [9]How "bad" were the children before they were spanked? [10]A _____ problem with research on spanking is understanding its impact as an element of a larger environment. [11]The households in which parents spank their children the most _____ tend, for example, to be households with more marital discord.

—Adapted from Gerrig, and Zimbardo, *Psychology and Life,* 18th ed., p. 184.

_____ 1. The best transition for the blank in sentence 6 is
    a. final.   c. often.
    b. another.   d. also.

_____ 2. The best transition for the blank in sentence 7 is
    a. final.   c. often.
    b. third.   d. also

_____ 3. The best transition for the blank in sentence 8 is
    a. final.   c. often.
    b. third.   d. also.

_____ 4. The best transition for the first blank in sentence 10 is
    a. final.   c. often.
    b. third.   d. also.

_____ 5. The best transition for the second blank in sentence 11 is
    a. final.   c. often.
    b. third.   d. also.

_____ 6. The thought pattern of this paragraph is
    a. listing.   c. classification.
    b. time order.   d. space order.

Directions: Read each set of sentences and answer the questions that follow.

One important choreographer of modern dance was José Limón (1908-1972), who formulated new techniques based on the dancer's relationship to gravity. _____ of great importance were the contributions of Alvin Ailey (1931–1989), founder in 1958 of the dance company that still bears his name.

—Adapted from Janaro and Altshuler, The Art of Being Human, 8th ed., pp. 330–331.

_____ 7. The best transition word for the sentence is
     a. first.   c. also.
     b. third.   d. final.

_____ 8. The relationship of the ideas between the two sentences is one of
     a. listing.   c. classification.
     b. time order.   d. space order.

The most popular organized exchange in the United States is the New York Stock Exchange (NYSE), which handles transactions for approximately 2,8000 stocks. _____ floor traders execute trades for other investors, they earn a commission, which reflects the difference between the price at which they are willing to buy a stock and the price at which they are willing to sell it.

—Adapted from Madura, Personal Finance, 3rd ed., p. 450.

_____ 9. The best transition word for the sentence is
     a. When.   c. Into.
     b. During.   d. First.

_____ 10. The relationship of the ideas between the two sentences is one of
     a. listing.   c. classification.
     b. time order.   d. space order.

Name _____ Section _____ Date _____ Score (number correct) _____ x 10 = _____

Objective: To use transition words to determine thought patterns.

Directions: Read the following paragraphs and answer the questions that follow.

A. Social pressures to maintain a lean body are great enough to encourage some people to under-eat, or to avoid foods they perceive as "bad," especially fats. Our society ridicules, and often snubs overweight people, many of whom even face job discrimination. Media images of thin fashion models and men in tight jeans with washboard abdomens and muscular chests encourage many people—especially adolescents and young adults—to skip meals, resort to crash diets, and exercise obsessively. Even some people of normal body weight push themselves to achieve an unrealistic and unattainable weight goal. This can often result in threatened health and even lives.

—Adapted from Thompson and Manore, Nutrition for Life, 2nd ed. p. 272.

_____ 1. The main thought pattern is _____.
    a. cause and effect
    b. comparison and contrast
    c. definition
    d. generalization and example

_____ 2. One transition word or phrase that signals the main thought pattern is _____.
    a. maintain
    b. ridicules
    c. even
    d. result

B. In the United States, young people expect to spend most of their first eighteen years in school. This was not the case a century ago, when just a small elite had the privilege of attending school. Even today, most young people in poor countries receive only a few years of formal schooling. The limited schooling that takes place in lower-income countries reflects the national culture. In Iran, for example, schooling is closely tied to Islam. Similarly, schooling in Bangladesh (Asia), Zimbabwe (Africa) and Nicaragua (Latin America) has been shaped by the distinctive cultural traditions of these nations. All lower-income countries have one trait in common when it comes to schooling: There is not much of it.

—Adapted from Macionis, Sociology, 13th ed., p. 516.

_____ 3. The main thought pattern is _____.
    a. cause and effect
    b. comparison and contrast
    c. definition
    d. generalization and example

135

_____ 4. One transition word or phrase that signals the main thought pattern is _____.
   a. when
   b. even
   c. similarly
   d. for example

C. Consumer loans are either secured or unsecured. A secured loan is defined as borrowed money that is guaranteed by a specific asset. If you can't meet the loan payments, that asset can be seized and sold to cover the amount due. Many times the asset purchased with the funds from the loan is used for security. For example, if you borrow money to buy a car, that car is generally used as collateral for the loan. If you don't make your car payment, your car maybe repossessed.

—Adapted from Keown, Personal Finance: Turning Money into Wealth, 5th ed., p. 196.

_____ 5. The main thought pattern is _____.
   a. cause and effect
   b. comparison and contrast
   c. definition
   d. generalization and example

_____ 6. One transition word or phrase that signals the main thought pattern is _____.
   a. is defined as
   b. times
   c. for example
   d. if

D. Toys made in the 1950's and 1960's are hot items that catch the eye of collectors. Carefully saving long-loved toys in our attics and closets often brings in income we never expected. Space toys and robots are two favorites that fetch high prices. In addition, original packages and tags, such as the original Barbie in an unopened box, may add enormously to the resale value of old toys.

_____ 7. The main thought pattern is _____.
   a. cause and effect
   b. comparison and contrast
   c. definition
   d. generalization and example

_____ 8. The word or phrase that signals the main thought pattern is _____.
   a. often
   b. brings in
   c. in addition
   d. such as

E. Elected members of the House of Representatives and the Senate have jobs with similar benefits. The first similarity is the salary; in 2002, each earned a salary of about $140,000 a year. Second, both receive generous retirement benefits. Third, both representatives and senators get large amounts of money to cover travel expenses. In addition, both groups have a fully staffed office in Washington and in their home which are paid for by tax dollars.

—Adapted from O'Connor and Sabato, American Government, Continuity and Change, p. 265

_____ 9. The main thought pattern is _____.
   a. cause and effect
   b. comparison
   c. contrast
   d. generalization and example

_____ 10. One transition word or phrase that signals the main thought pattern is _____.
   a. first
   b. benefits
   c. similar
   d. in addition

Chapter 10: More Thought Patterns
LAB 10.2 PRACTICE EXERCISE 2

Name _____ Section _____ Date _____ Score (number correct) _____ x 10 = _____

Objective: To use transition words to determine thought patterns.

Directions: Read the following paragraphs and answer the questions that follow.

A. In today's world, humans are the primary cause of erosion, and we have accelerated erosion to unnaturally high rates. In a 2004 study, one geologist analyzed prehistoric erosion rates and compared these with modern rates. He concluded that human activities move over 10 times more soil than all other natural processes on the surface of the planet combined.

Adapted from Withgott and Brennan, *Essential Environment: The Science Behind the Stories*, 3rd ed. p. 138.

_____ 1. The main thought pattern is
    a. cause and effect.
    b. comparison and contrast.
    c. definition.
    d. generalization and example.

_____ 2. One transition word or phrase that signals the main thought pattern is
    a. today's.　　　　　　　　　c. compared.
    b. cause.　　　　　　　　　　d. than.

B. Reading a book is always much better than watching a movie based on a book. Despite the saying, "A picture is worth a thousand words," a book is able to give much more information than a movie can give. The author can give the thoughts of the characters; in contrast, a movie usually conveys only the actions and words of the characters. A book can follow several characters and plot lines, but a movie usually has fewer than two hours to tell the story and must follow just a few characters or one plot line. The final difference is one of imagination. Each reader of a book can create a different mental picture of the characters and scenes. A movie, however, can offer only the vision of the director and actors.

_____ 3. The main thought pattern is
    a. cause and effect.
    b. comparison.
    c. contrast.
    d. generalization and example.

_____ 4. One transition word or phrase that signals the main thought pattern is
    a. in contrast.　　　　　　　c. and.
    b. follow.　　　　　　　　　d. final.

C. The true joy of learning comes from the "eureka" experience. "Eureka" refers to that moment when real understanding breaks through the confusion and one knows one has learned something. For example, Kim had worked for weeks on her spelling. One day when she wasn't even thinking about spelling, the link between sounds and letters suddenly became very clear. With that burst of understanding, she knew instantly how to spell many words that had puzzled her before. She was thrilled.

138

_____ 5. The main thought pattern is
    a. cause and effect.   c. contrast.
    b. comparison.   d. definition.

_____ 6. One transition word or phrase that signals the main thought pattern is
    a. true.   c. one day.
    b. refers to.   d. with.

D. Of 115 marine mammal species, 49 are known to have eaten or become entangled in marine debris, and 111 of 312 species of seabirds are known to ingest plastic. All five species of sea turtle in the Gulf of Mexico have died from consuming or contacting marine debris. Marine debris affects people, as well. A survey of fishers off the Oregon coast indicated that more than half had encountered equipment damage or other problems from plastic debris, and debris has caused over $50 million dollars in insurance payments. In December 2006, the U.S. Congress responded to these threats and passed the Marine Debris Research, Prevention, and Reduction Act.

        —Withgott and Brennan, *Environment: The Science behind the Stories*, 3rd ed., p. 455.

_____ 7. The main thought pattern is
    a. cause and effect.
    b. comparison and contrast.
    c. definition.
    d. generalization and example.

_____ 8. Words or a phrase that signal the main thought pattern are
    a. are known.   c. affects; causes.
    b. all five.   d. a survey.

E. Two important differences between the treatment of men and that of women persist in military service. First, only men must register for the draft when they turn 18. Second, statutes and regulations also prohibit women from serving in combat. A breach exists between policy and practice, however, as the Persian Gulf War and the war in Iraq showed. Women piloted helicopters at the front and helped to operate antimissile systems; some were taken as prisoners of war. Women are now permitted to serve as combat pilots in the navy and air force and to serve on navy warships. However, they are still not permitted to serve in ground combat units in the army or marines.

        —Adapted from Edwards, Wattenberg, and Lineberry, *Government in America: People, Politics, and Policy,* 13th ed., p. 162.

_____ 9. The main thought pattern is
    a. cause and effect.   c. definition.
    b. contrast.   d. generalization.

_____ 10. Words or a phrase that signal the main thought pattern are
    a. differences; however.   c. now.
    b. first; second.   d. also.

Chapter 10: More Thought Patterns
LAB 10.3 REVIEW TEST 1

Name _____ Section _____ Date _____ Score (number correct) _____ x 10 = _____

Directions: Read the following paragraphs and answer the questions that follow.

A. Developing a strong mind is just like developing a strong body. Both require commitment and hard work. Just as the muscles in the body must be repeatedly worked to get stronger, so must the mind. So, just as one would lift weights three times a week for so many repetitions, one would also set aside time to read. As the body builds up muscles, likewise the mind builds up knowledge. Another similarity lies in developing memory. A person who exercises regularly develops muscle memory. It doesn't take long for the body to bounce back into shape because the muscles respond more quickly if they have been trained. The same is true of the mind. The mind remembers what it has practiced and is ready to pick up on new information.

_____ 1. The main thought pattern is
   a. cause and effect.
   b. comparison and contrast.
   c. definition.
   d. generalization and example.

_____ 2. Words that signal the main thought pattern are
   a. both; similarity.
   b. / so; if.
   c. also; another.
   d. ready; long.

B. Some of the greatest lessons I have ever learned came as a result of humiliation or suffering. First, I had to learn how to forgive because my peers in third grade made fun of me by giving me the nickname "Dork." Second, I learned to be patient as the result of working for three years to save enough money to buy my first car. Third, I learned to be honest because I was caught in a lie that didn't even need to be told. Finally, I learned to say "I love you" to those I love as a result of my father's dying before I could tell him how much he meant to me.

_____ 3. The main thought pattern is
   a. cause and effect.
   b. comparison and contrast.
   c. definition.
   d. generalization and example.

_____ 4. Words or a phrase that signal the main thought pattern are
   a. some.
   b. first; second; finally.
   c. as a result; because.
   d. before.

C. Learning to be a successful college student involves adopting a positive attitude and consistently practicing strategies that lead to success. For example, regular study sessions throughout a course will heighten a feeling of accomplishment and diminish feelings of stress when it comes to exam time. Those students who learn to take effective notes, develop study cards, and rehearse knowledge until they can repeat it aloud, discover the joy and freedom from anxiety that good study skills create.

_____ 5. The main thought pattern is
   a. cause and effect.
   b. comparison and contrast.
   c. definition.
   d. generalization and example.

_____ 6. The word or phrase that signals the main thought pattern is
   a. lead to.   c. time.
   b. for example.   d. when; until.

D. The British Empire banned slavery in 1833, followed by the United States in 1865. On the other hand slavery is a reality for at least 20 million men, women, and children and as many as 200 million people live in conditions that come close to slavery. One form of slavery is human trafficking, which is the moving of men, women, and children from one place to another for the purpose of performing forced labor. Women or men are brought to a new country with the promise of a job and then forced to become prostitutes or farm laborers. Sometimes "parents" adopt children from another country and then force them to work in sweatshops. Such activity is big business. Next to trading in guns and drugs, trading in people brings the greatest profit to organized crime around the world.

—Adapted from Macionis, *Sociology*, 13th ed., p. 310.

_____ 7. The main thought pattern is
   a. cause and effect.
   b. comparison and contrast.
   c. definition.
   d. generalization and example .

_____ 8. Words or a phrase that signal the main thought pattern are _____
   a. on the other hand.
   b. which is.
   c. one form.
   d. for the purpose

E. People with bulimia often binge and then take inappropriate measures, such as secret vomiting (purging), to lose the calories they have just acquired. Up to three percent of adolescents and young female adults are bulimic, with male rates being about ten percent of the female rate. Just like people who are anorexic, people with bulimia are also obsessed with their bodies, weight gain, and how they appear to others. Unlike those with anorexia, people with bulimia are often "hidden" from the public eye because their weight may vary only slightly or fall within a normal range. Also, treatment appears to be more effective for bulimia than for anorexia.

—Adapted from Donatelle, *Access to Health*, 10th ed., pp. 312–313.

_____ 9. The main thought pattern is
    a. cause and effect.   c. definition.
    b. comparison and contrast.   d. generalization and example.

_____ 10. A word or a phrase that signals the main thought pattern is
    a. just like; unlike.   c. because.
    b. often.   d. also.

Chapter 10: More Thought Patterns
LAB 10.4 REVIEW TEST 2

Name _____ Section_____ Date_____Score (number correct) _____ x 10 = _____

Directions: Read the following paragraphs and answer the questions that follow.

A. Back in 1900, about one-third of all deaths in the United States occurred before the age of five and fully two-thirds before the age of fifty-five. As societies gradually learned more about health and medicine, death became less of an everyday experience. Fewer children died at birth, and accidents and disease took a smaller toll among adults. As a result, most people living in high-income societies today view dying as extraordinary, something that happens to the very old or to younger people in rare and tragic cases.

—Adapted from Macionis, *Sociology*, 13th ed., p. 401.

_____1. The main thought pattern is _____
    a. cause and effect.
    b. comparison and contrast.
    c. definition.
    d. generalization and example.

_____2. A word or phrase that signals the main thought pattern is _____
    a. back.
    b. as.
    c. fewer.
    d. as a result.

B. Environmental factors present in our childhood can influence our food choices, activity level, and other behaviors as adults. For example, children who are very physically active and eat healthful diets are less likely to be overweight or obese as children. In contrast, children who spend most of their time on the computer or watching television and who eat a lot of foods that contain excess fat and sugar are more likely to be overweight or obese as children. And we know that being overweight as a child can be harmful to our health as we age.

—Adapted from Thompson and Manore, *Nutrition for Life*, 2nd ed., p. 268.

_____3. The main thought pattern is _____
    a. cause and effect.
    b. comparison and contrast.
    c. definition.
    d. generalization and example.

_____4. A word or phrase that signals the main thought pattern is _____
    a. factors.
    b. for example.
    c. in contrast.
    d. and.

C. *Training* can be defined as activity leading to skilled behavior. Training is very specific to any given activity or goal. For instance, if you want to train for athletic competition, a traditional approach that includes planned, purposeful exercise sessions under the guidance of a trainer or coach would probably be most beneficial. An example of this is participating in an aerobics class at least 3 times a week, or jogging for at least 20 minutes 3 times a week if you want to achieve cardio-respiratory fitness.

—Adapted from Thompson and Manore, *Nutrition for Life*, 2nd ed., p. 305.

_____5. The main thought pattern is _____
    a. cause and effect.
    b. comparison and contrast.
    c. definition.
    d. generalization and example.

_____6. A word or phrase that signals the main thought pattern is _____
    a. generally.
    b. is defined
    c. for instance.
    d. for example.

D. Although pollution has flowed in the Tijuana River for at least 70 years, the problem has grown worse in recent years. This river pollution directly affects people's day-to-day lives. Mexican residents who reside along the Tijuana River live in poverty compared to their American neighbors on the other side. Close to one-third of these homes are not connected to a sewer system. During periods of heavy rainfall, leaky sewer systems become clogged with debris, causing raw sewage to overflow into the streets. In addition, the rise of American factories on the Mexican side of the border has contributed to the river's pollution, both through direct disposal of industrial waste and by attracting thousands of new workers to the already crowded region.

—Adapted from Withgott and Brennan, *Essential Environment: The Science Behind the Stories*, 3rd ed., p. 24.

_____7. The main thought pattern is _____
    a. cause and effect.
    b. comparison and contrast.
    c. definition.
    d. generalization and example.

_____8. A word or words that signal the main thought pattern are _____
    a. compared.
    b. during.
    c. in addition.
    d. affects, causing, contributed.

E. Private boarding schools provide an outstanding education, and the independent living experience helps students prepare for success in a good college or university For example, Lawrenceville School in New Jersey has small classes with extremely well-trained and very dedicated teachers. This magnificent campus has facilities that rival those of the nation's top colleges. The cost for a single year at such a school is about $50,000 for most students. Liberal Democrats such as the Obamas strongly support public education, but they, like most other residents of the White House, have chosen private schooling for their children.

—Adapted from Macionis, *Sociology*, 13th ed., p. 536.

_____ 9. The main thought pattern is _____
   a. cause and effect.
   b. comparison and contrast.
   c. definition.
   d. generalization and example.

_____ 10. A word or words that signal the main thought pattern are _____
   a. for example.
   b. extremely.
   c. magnificent.
   d. but.

Name _____ Section _____ Date ____,_____Score (number correct) _____ x 10 = _____

Directions: Read the following paragraphs and answer the questions that follow.

A. Many people believe that men and women make decisions very differently. It is believed that men do not allow their emotions to affect their decisions. Men are thought to focus on actions and behaviors, and they seem to measure success by results. In contrast, it is believed that women rely heavily on their feelings as they work through a decision. Women, unlike men, are thought to focus more on motives than on behaviors. In addition, women, it would seem, value what is learned or gained in the process rather than the result.

_____ 1. The main thought pattern is
     a.   cause and effect.
     b.   contrast.
     c.   definition.
     d.   generalization and example.

_____ 2. Words that signal the main thought pattern are
     a.   many; their.
     b.   and; in addition.
     c.   affect; results.
     d.   in contrast; unlike.

B. A good credit rating results from following a few simple rules. Apply for and use a single credit card in order to obtain good credit. Keeping track of what you charge and keeping up with the payments on time will cause lenders to believe that you are responsible. Another rule is that paying off your credit-card bill each month will lead to good credit. The zero balance that results tells lenders that you know how to manage your money.

_____ 3. The main thought pattern is
     a.   cause and effect.
     b.   comparison and contrast.
     c.   definition.
     d.   generalization and example.

_____ 4. A word or a phrase that signals the main thought pattern is
     a.   another.
     b.   few.
     c.   as a result; because.
     d.   on time.

C. Like animals, humans mark both their primary and secondary territories to signal ownership Some teenagers—perhaps because they can't yet own territories—use markers to indicate pseudo-ownership or appropriation of someone else's space, or of a public territory, for their own use. Graffiti and the markings of gang boundaries come quickly to mind as examples. Also, like animals, humans use territory to signal their status. For example, the size and location of your territory (your home or office, say,) indicates something about your status. Higher-status individuals have a "right" to invade the territory of lower-status persons, but the reverse is not true. The boss of a large company, for example, can barge into the office of a junior executive, but the reverse would be unthinkable. Similarly, a teacher may invade a student's personal space by looking over her or his shoulder as the student writes, but the student cannot do the same to the teacher.

—Adapted from DeVito, *The Interpersonal Communication Book*, 11th ed. pp. 181–182.

_____ 5. The main thought pattern is
    a. cause and effect.
    b. comparison.
    c. contrast.
    d. definition.

_____ 6. A word or phrase that signals the main thought pattern is
    a. but.   c. similarly.
    b. for example.   d. but.

D. People have long made the oceans a sink for waste and pollution. For example, even into the mid-20th century, it was common for coastal U.S. cities to dump trash and untreated sewage along their shores. Fort Bragg, a bustling town on the northern California coast, boasts of its Glass Beach, an area where beachcombers collect sea glass, the colorful surf-polished glass sometimes found on beaches after storms. Oil, plastic, industrial chemicals, and excess nutrients are other examples of contaminants that eventually make their way from land into the oceans.

—Withgott and Brennan, *Essential Environment: The Science Behind the Stories*, 3rd ed., p. 455.

_____ 7. The main thought pattern is
    a. cause and effect.
    b. comparison and contrast.
    c. definition.
    d. generalization and example.

_____ 8. A word or phrase that signals the main thought pattern is
    a. for example.   c. sometimes.
    b. along.   d. eventually.

E. Biofeedback is a self-regulatory technique used for a variety of special applications. As pioneered by psychologist Neal Miller, biofeedback is a procedure that makes an individual aware of ordinarily weak or internal responses by providing clear external signals. The patient is allowed to "see" his or her own bodily reactions, which are monitored and amplified by equipment that transforms them into lights and sound cues of varying intensity. The patient's task is then to control the level of these external cues. Some examples of applications of biofeedback include helping patients control blood pressure, stop tension headaches, and even diminish extreme blushing.

—Adapted from Gerrig and Zimbardo, *Psychology and Life,* 18th ed., p. 408.

_____ 9. The main thought pattern is
      a. cause and effect.
      b. comparison and contrast.
      c. definition and example.
      d. generalization and example.

_____ 10. A word or a phrase that signals the main thought pattern is
      a. as.
      b. then.
      c. some examples.
      d. include.

Chapter 10: More Thought Patterns
LAB 10.6 MASTERY TEST 2

Name _____ Section _____ Date _____ Score (number correct) _____ x 10 = _____

Directions: Read the following paragraphs and answer the questions that follow.

A. There are those among us who have faced and overcome terrible tragedies or horrible difficulties. These "overcomers" rise above their situations for a number of reasons. One reason they overcome is that they look for the good in the bad. They remain sure that a lesson can be learned from the worst of circumstances. Second, they overcome because they use the lessons they learn to help others. Because they are determined to reject bitterness, they look for ways to share their hard-earned wisdom with others who may be facing similar difficulties. Finally, these remarkable people usually rely on a deep faith in a higher power. They trust that even in suffering, there is a purpose. Their trust and faith lead them to seek both the lessons in pain and the opportunities to help others.

_____ 1. The main thought pattern is
   a. cause and effect.
   b. comparison and contrast.
   c. definition.
   d. generalization and example.

_____ 2. Words that signal the main thought pattern are
   a. one; second; finally.
   b. both; and.
   c. reasons; because.
   d. similar difficulties.

B. Apart from the obvious effects, sexual abuse subtly affects the lifelong behavior of the abused child. One subtle effect is the lifetime struggle to learn how to trust others. Many times, the offender is someone the child knows and trusts. Sexual abuse violates this trust in the most dreadful way. Thus distrust takes root early. Shame and fear on the part of the victim often keep the child silent about the abuse, and this silence may lead to repeated attacks by the abuser. Therefore, the distrust becomes deeply rooted and shoots off into other parts of the victim's life. Long-term results may include a distrust of oneself, the opposite sex, and authority figures.

_____ 3. The main thought pattern is
   a. cause and effect.
   b. comparison.
   c. contrast.
   d. definition.

_____ 4. A word or phrase that signals the main thought pattern is
   a. one.   c. effect.
   b. many times.   d. may.

149

C. Contrary to the image promoted in the media of the police officer as primarily engaged in crime fighting, the reality of police work is that most police officers spend only a small portion of their time in crime-fighting activities. Unlike the police officers in television series who receive misdemeanor and felony calls on each episode, most real police officers are more likely to receive numerous calls for service and order maintenance. It is not uncommon for officers to complete a shift without making any arrests for criminal behavior.

—Adapted from Fagin, *Criminal Justice,* 2nd ed., p. 255.

_____ 5. The main thought pattern is
   a. cause and effect.
   b. comparison.
   c. contrast.
   d. generalization and example.

_____ 6. A word or a phrase that signals the main thought pattern is
   a. contrary.
   b. few.
   c. as a result; because.
   d. on time.

D. Besides expressing a wider range of emotions, infants and toddlers begin to manage their emotional experiences. Emotional self-regulation refers to the strategies we use to adjust our emotional state to a comfortable level of intensity so we can accomplish our goal. For example, when you remind yourself that an anxiety-provoking event will be over soon, suppress your anger at a friend's behavior, or decide not to see a scary horror film, you are engaging in emotional self-regulation.

—Adapted from Berk, *Development Through the Lifespan,* 4th ed., p. 189.

_____ 7. The main thought pattern is
   a. cause and effect.
   b. comparison and contrast.
   c. definition.
   d. generalization and example.

_____ 8. A word or phrase that signals the main thought pattern is
   a. besides.
   b. refers to.
   c. so.
   d. soon.

E. You should safeguard your personal information and make it harder for an identity thief to prey on you. Most of these safeguards are relatively easy and inexpensive. For example, simply by removing anything that contains your Social Security number, including your Social Security card, from your wallet or purse, is one of the easiest forms of protection you can take. You should never carry, unless absolutely necessary, your passport, birth certificate, and rarely-used credit cards. Also be sure that you are not carrying any account passwords or PINs in your wallet.

_____ 9. The main thought pattern is
   a. cause and effect.
   b. comparison and contrast.
   c. definition.
   d. generalization and example.

_____10. A word or phrase that signals the main thought pattern is
   a. should.
   b. for example.
   c. one.
   d. also.

Chapter 11: Inferences
LAB 11.1 PRACTICE EXERCISE 1

Name _____ Section _____ Date _____ Score (number correct) _____ x 10 = _____

Objective: To identify inferences that are valid.

Directions: Read the following paragraphs and decide if each inference is supported by the details in the paragraph.

A. Mandy, I've given your essay a C grade for several reasons. First, it contained many grammar and usage errors. In addition to making spelling errors, you often confused words like *there* and *their*. Your sentences were all complete, but they lacked variety—you used only one kind of sentence. You also used informal word choices such as *a lot of* instead of *many* and *kids* instead of *children*. Your essay did offer a main idea and major supporting details. However, the details were just listed instead of explained. I am certain that if you focus on these matters in the future, your writing will be much improved.

_____1. Everything about the student's essay is weak.
   a. Yes, this is a valid inference.
   b. No, this is not a valid inference.

_____2. The student writer needs to proofread her essays.
   a. Yes, this is a valid inference.
   b. No, this is not a valid inference.

_____3. The student writer has a good vocabulary.
   a. Yes, this is a valid inference.
   b. No, this is not a valid inference.

_____4. The student writer needs to work on her spelling skills.
   a. Yes, this is a valid inference.
   b. No, this is not a valid inference.

_____5. The student writer needs to work on adding more variety to her writing.
   a. Yes, this is a valid inference.
   b. No, this is not a valid inference.

B. [1]Two students enter a classroom. [2]The first student, Philip, pauses just inside the doorway with a piece of paper in his hand. [3]He looks around, looks at the paper, and looks around again with a puzzled frown. [4]He repeats this action a few times. [5]Then, without speaking to anyone, he quickly takes a seat in the back of the room near the door. [6]He does not have any books, but he does have a pen and a notepad. [7]He fidgets in his seat as he waits for class to begin. [8]The second student, Clara, walks with assurance to take a seat in the front row. [9]As she chats with the people around her, she unzips her backpack and pulls out the textbook *College Math,* a notebook, and a tape recorder. [10]Then she settles into her seat, opens her textbook to the current assignment, and pulls out her homework. [11]The teacher enters the room. [12]As he takes the attendance, he introduces Philip to the rest of the class. [13]The teacher also takes time to tell Philip where to purchase the textbook for the course. [14]After class, Clara introduces herself to Philip and offers to show him how to get to the bookstore.

_____6. Choose the inference that is supported by the details in sentences 2-4.
     a. Philip is confused and unsure.
     b. Philip is shy.

_____7. Choose the inference that is supported by the details in sentence 5.
     a. Philip is rude.
     b. Philip wants to be close to the exit.

_____8. Choose the inference that is supported by the details in sentence 9.
     a. The two students are in college.
     b. The two students know each other.

_____9. Choose the inference that is supported by the details in sentence 14.
     a. Clara is friendly and helpful.
     b. Clara wants to go out on a date with Philip.

_____10. Choose the inference that is supported by the overall details in the passage.
     a. Philip is a poor student who comes to class unprepared.
     b. Philip is unsure because he is a new student.

Chapter 11: Inferences
LAB 11.2 PRACTICE EXERCISE 2

Name _____ Section _____ Date _____ Score (number correct) _____ x 10 = _____

Objective: To identify inferences that are valid.

Directions: Read the following paragraphs and decide if each inference is supported by the details in the paragraph.

A. *Casablanca* (1942) became immortal almost in spite of itself. Each day the scriptwriters gave revised scenes to the cast, who made fun of the whole venture when the day's shooting was over. None of them knew how the film would end, and almost everyone thought it would be a disastrous failure. The United States had just entered World War II, the outcome of which was by no means certain. War movies abounded in Hollywood, most of them filled with multiple scenes of artillery fire, bombings, and mine explosions. Audiences were given Allied successes on the battlefield and reason to cheer. Yet *Casablanca*, despite its wartime background, lacked the expected action scenes. Somehow, through revision after revision, it became a powerful story about one man's ethical dilemma at a time of conflicting moral values.

—Adapted from Janaro and Altshuler, *The Art of Being Human,* 8th ed., p. 375.

_____ 1. Casablanca was deemed a raging success from the first day of shooting.
     a. Yes, this is a valid inference.
     b. No, this is not a valid inference.

_____ 2. The actors had memorized their lines months before the movie was filmed.
     a. Yes, this is a valid inference.
     b. No, this is not a valid inference.

_____ 3. Casablanca was a disastrous failure.
     a. Yes, this is a valid inference.
     b. No, this is not a valid inference.

_____ 4. Casablanca had few action-packed battle scenes compared to most other war movies of its time.
     a. Yes, this is a valid inference.
     b. No, this is not a valid inference.

_____ 5. The writers of Casablanca made many modifications to the script as it was being filmed.
     a. Yes, this is a valid inference.
     b. No, this is not a valid inference.

B. People who feel that the costs of some dams have outweighed their benefits are pushing for such dams to be dismantled. By removing dams and letting rivers flow freely, these people say, we can restore ecosystems, re-establish economically valuable fisheries, and revive river recreation such as fly-fishing and rafting. Increasingly, private dam owners and the Federal Energy Regulatory Commission, the U.S. government agency charged with renewing licenses for dams, have agreed. Roughly 500 dams have been removed in the United States in recent years. One reason is that many aging dams are in need of costly repairs or have outlived their economic usefulness.

—Adapted from Withgott and Brennan, *Environment: The Science behind the Stories*, 3rd ed., p. 421

_____ 6. The damming of American rivers has created some environmental problems.
    a. Yes, this is a valid inference.
    b. No, this is not a valid inference.

_____ 7. The effectiveness of dams is being scrutinized.
    a. Yes, this is a valid inference.
    b. No, this is not a valid inference.

_____ 8. Anyone can build and own a dam.
    a. Yes, this is a valid inference.
    b. No, this is not a valid inference.

_____ 9. Removing dams will help restore fish to rivers.
    a. Yes, this is a valid inference.
    b. No, this is not a valid inference.

_____ 10. People are beginning to question the value of many dams.
    a. Yes, this is a valid inference.
    b. No, this is not a valid inference.

Name _____ Section_____ Date _____ Score (number correct) _____ x 10 = _____

Directions: Read the following paragraphs and decide if each inference is supported by the details in the paragraph.

A. The advantages of bilingualism provide strong justification for bilingual education programs in schools. In Canada, about seven percent of elementary school students are enrolled in language immersion programs, in which English-speaking children are taught entirely in French for several years. This strategy has been successful in developing children who are proficient in both languages and who, by grade six, achieve as well as their counterparts in the regular English program. Canadian schools are also encouraged to provide programs that maintain the languages and cultures of immigrants and to promote First Nations languages, such as those spoken by the native-born people. Although such programs are in short supply, funding for them is increasing.

—Adapted from Berk, *Development Through the Lifespan,* 4th ed., p. 318

_____ 1. Children can learn in two different languages at the same time.
    a. Yes, this is a valid inference.
    b. No, this is not a valid inference.

_____ 2. Children who are bilingual perform just as well as those who are not, after several years of learning a language.
    a. Yes, this is a valid inference.
    b. No, this is not a valid inference.

_____ 3. Children in language-immersion programs are not expected to learn the content of courses such as geography, science, or health. They are expected to merely learn the language.
    a. Yes, this is a valid inference.
    b. No, this is not a valid inference.

_____ 4. The regular school curriculum is taught through the medium of a foreign language in a language immersion program.
    a. Yes, this is a valid inference.
    b. No, this is not a valid inference.

_____ 5. The Irish language is an example of a First Nations language.
    a. Yes, this is a valid inference.
    b. No, this is not a valid inference

B. A major concern of the criminal justice and juvenile justice system is child pornography. Child pornography is closely related to sexual abuse of children because (1) the production of the material frequently involves children as victims, as often the child molester produces his own child pornography, and (2) child sex offenders almost always collect child pornography. In contrast to adult pornography, but consistent with the gender preference of many pedophiles, there is a high percentage of boys in child pornography. Unlike adult pornography, which may be considered immoral but legal by some laws, child pornography is universally illegal. However, there is no legal definition of child pornography common to all states and federal law.

—Adapted from Fagin, *Criminal Justice,* 2nd ed., p. 627.

_____ 6. Adult pornography may be considered legal.
   a. Yes, this is a valid inference.
   b. No, this is not a valid inference.

_____ 7. Boys are more frequently pictured in child pornography than girls.
   a. Yes, this is a valid inference.
   b. No, this is not a valid inference.

_____ 8. All those who collect and view child pornography are probably child sex offenders.
   a. Yes, this is a valid inference.
   b. No, this is not a valid inference.

_____ 9. Possessing child pornography is illegal.
   a. Yes, this is a valid inference.
   b. No, this is not a valid inference.

_____ 10. Distributing child pornography over the Internet is illegal.
   a. Yes, this is a valid inference.
   b. No, this is not a valid inference.

Name _____ Section _____ Date _____ Score (number correct) _____ x 10 = _____

Directions: Read the following paragraphs and decide if each inference is supported by the details in the paragraph.

Paul Booth, Tattoo Artist

A. Click into tattoo artist Paul Booth's Web site, darkimages.com, and enter the dark side of tattoo art. Known world-wide for his macabre art drawn on human flesh, Booth advertises himself as the "Dark Overlord and Master of the cruel alternative reality" called Last Rites, his popular and highly successful tattoo studio located in New York's East Village. His own body is a walking testament to his passion for body art. Booth's five feet nine, stocky frame sports tattoos from shoulders to hands; multiple silver rings rim his ears, and a single silver loop hangs from his nose. His clean-shaven head, except for the thick mass of long hair left to grow from its center back, serves as a canvas for a coiled centipede design that covers the skin over his right skull and creeps down his neck. Interestingly, his studio, described as "an asylum for dark creatures to gather and be marked," sits across the street from a Catholic church that is adorned with cheerful and colorful murals of birthday cakes created by children.

_____1. Paul Booth is a successful businessman.
    a. Yes, this is a valid inference
    b. No, this is not a valid inference

_____2. To many, tattooing is a form of art.
    a. Yes, this is a valid inference
    b. No, this is not a valid inference

_____3. Paul Booth is dangerous.
    a. Yes, this is a valid inference
    b. No, this is not a valid inference

_____4. Paul Booth is very wealthy because most people prefer a tattoo comprised of a cruel image.
    a. Yes, this is a valid inference
    b. No, this is not a valid inference

_____5. The Catholic church across the street probably denounces Paul Booth and his business.
    a. Yes, this is a valid inference
    b. No, this is not a valid inference

Who's the Fairest?

B. The goddess of love, Aphrodite, was the most beautiful of all the Greek goddesses. In fact, her beauty was so great that two other goddesses, Hera and Athena, became quite jealous of her. Hera and Athena demanded a contest for the title of the "fairest." Zeus, the king of the gods, appointed a mortal man, Paris, to judge the contest. All three goddesses tried to bribe Paris. Aphrodite promised Paris that she could make the most beautiful woman on earth fall in love with him. Her bribe worked, and she won the title. To keep her end of the bargain, Aphrodite gave Helen of Troy (the world's most beautiful woman) to Paris. Hera and Athena became very angry when they didn't win the contest. To get even with Aphrodite and Paris, these two angry goddesses caused the Greeks to make war on Paris, his family, and his country. In the end, Paris lost everything, including his life.

_____6. Greek gods and goddesses behaved very much like humans.
   a. Yes, this is a valid inference
   b. No, this is not a valid inference

_____7. Paris was in love with Aphrodite.
   a. Yes, this is a valid inference
   b. No, this is not a valid inference

_____ 8. Aphrodite did not win the title fairly.
   a. Yes, this is a valid inference
   b. No, this is not a valid inference

_____9. Hera, Athena, and Aphrodite were not concerned about the well-being of humans.
   a. Yes, this is a valid inference
   b. No, this is not a valid inference

_____10. In the eyes of the Greeks, mortal men are fairer when it comes to judging beauty contests.
   a. Yes, this is a valid inference
   b. No, this is not a valid inference

Name _____ Section_____ Date_____Score (number correct) _____ x 10 = _____

Directions: Read the following paragraphs and decide if each inference is supported by the details in the paragraph.

A. The average American has a life expectancy of 77 years—a high number, but one surpassed by citizens of most other developed nations. Despite the advances in medical technology, the average American does not live as long as the average Canadian. Using a measure of healthy longevity, the World Health Organization ranked the United States twenty-fourth among the world's nations. The second common indicator of a healthy population is its infant mortality rate, the chances that a baby will die before its crucial first year. The chances in the United State of a baby's dying in the first year of life are more than 50 percent higher than those of a baby born in Japan. Indeed, the United States ranks only eighteenth among the world's nations in infant mortality. The health-care system in the Unites States may be part of the explanation.

—Adapted from Edwards, Wattenberg, and Lineberry, *Government in America: People, Politics, and Policy,* 12th ed., pp. 588–589.

_____ 1. Americans enjoy the best health care in the world.
    a. Yes, this is a valid inference.
    b. No, this is not a valid inference.

_____ 2. Infants have a better chance of surviving in Japan than they do in America.
    a. Yes, this is a valid inference.
    b. No, this is not a valid inference.

_____ 3. The American health-care system is considered to be superior to health care around the world.
    a. Yes, this is a valid inference.
    b. No, this is not a valid inference.

_____ 4. Americans live longer than do citizens of most other developed countries.
    a. Yes, this is a valid inference.
    b. No, this is not a valid inference.

_____ 5. Canadians have a longer life-expectancy rate than do Americans.
    a. Yes, this is a valid inference.
    b. No, this is not a valid inference.

B. A photograph of Earth reveals a great deal, but it does not convey the complexity of our environment. Our environment includes all the living and nonliving things around us with which we interact. It includes the continents, oceans, clouds, and ice caps you can see in the photo of Earth from space, as well as the animals, plants, forests, and farms that comprise the landscapes around us. In a more inclusive sense, it also encompasses our built environment—the structures, urban centers, and living spaces that people have created. In its most inclusive sense, our environment also includes the complex webs of social relationships and institutions that shape our daily lives.

People commonly use the term environment in the first, most narrow sense—to mean a nonhuman or "natural" world apart from human society. This usage is unfortunate, because it masks the very important fact that humans exist within the environment and are part of nature. As one of many species on Earth, we share with others the same dependence on a healthy, functioning planet. The limitations of language make it all too easy to speak of "people and nature," or "human society and the environment," as though they were separate and did not interact. However, the fundamental insight of environmental science is that we are part of the natural world and that our interactions with its other parts matter a great deal.

—Withgott and Brennan, Environment: The Science behind the Stories, 3rd ed., p. 3.

_____ 6. Families, work friends, churches, and other social groups are not considered part of our environment.
   a. Yes, this is a valid inference.
   b. No, this is not a valid inference.

_____ 7. Our environment is the sum total of our surroundings.
   a. Yes, this is a valid inference.
   b. No, this is not a valid inference.

_____ 8. The elements of our environment were functioning long before the human species appeared.
   a. Yes, this is a valid inference.
   b. No, this is not a valid inference.

_____ 9. Humans must be considered as separate from nature when studying the environment.
   a. Yes, this is a valid inference.
   b. No, this is not a valid inference.

_____ 10. Because buildings, roads, and bridges are man-made structures and not part of the original landscape, they should not be considered as part of the environment.
   a. Yes, this is a valid inference.
   b. No, this is not a valid inference.

Chapter 11: Inferences
LAB 11.6 MASTERY TEST 2

Name _____ Section _____ Date _____ Score (number correct) _____ x 10 = _____

Directions: Read the following paragraphs and decide if each inference is supported by the details in the paragraph.

A. China is the world's fastest growing economy, roaring along at the astounding growth rate of ten percent a year. China is also one of America's biggest trading partners. If Wal-Mart were a separate nation, it would rank as China's fifth-largest trading partner, ahead of Germany and Britain. With 1.3 billion people, China has the world's largest population as well. Over the centuries, however, Chinese governments have been among the world's most totalitarian. Human rights groups annually document the jailing of union and religious leaders and political dissidents. China's critics claim that its government-owned factories rely on slave labor to keep low labor costs even lower.

—Adapted from Edwards, Wattenberg, and Lineberry, *Government in America: People, Politics, and Policy,* 12th ed., p. 559.

_____ 1. China's government is considered one of the most democratic, very similar to America's government.
   a. Yes, this is a valid inference.
   b. No, this is not a valid inference.

_____ 2. Wal-Mart will probably be established as a separate country within the United States.
   a. Yes, this is a valid inference.
   b. No, this is not a valid inference.

_____ 3. People who openly oppose the government in China risk being placed into prison.
   a. Yes, this is a valid inference.
   b. No, this is not a valid inference.

_____ 4. China supports the use of slavery.
   a. Yes, this is a valid inference.
   b. No, this is not a valid inference.

_____ 5. China's economy is growing at a faster pace than America's economy is growing.
   a. Yes, this is a valid inference.
   b. No, this is not a valid inference.

B. The stories in musical film were often similar to those in romantic comedy. The couple were kept apart until the final embrace, except they sang and danced together. This formula was especially true for Fred Astaire and Ginger Rogers, who, even though their characters had different names in each film, always played essentially the same people. Once again the clothing and sets were lavish. Impeccably garbed Fred, with top hat and tails, and sleek, satin-gowned Ginger, with sequins and feathers, danced up and down stairs, on tabletops, and even on miraculously cleared dance floors in intricately choreographed routines (even though the script may indicate they have just met and obviously had no time to rehearse). No matter what minor misunderstanding may have separated them, when the band began to play, the story stopped as they tapped, waltzed, swirled, and introduced new rhythms.

—Janaro and Altshuler, *The Art of Being Human,* 8th ed., p. 356.

_____ 6. Ginger Rogers and Fred Astaire starred in many movies together.
   a. Yes, this is a valid inference.
   b. No, this is not a valid inference.

_____ 7. Numerous films continued the same story of Ginger and Fred's characters as they danced through life.
   a. Yes, this is a valid inference.
   b. No, this is not a valid inference.

_____ 8. The couples in musical films usually fell in love at first sight, but most often end in tragic separation.
   a. Yes, this is a valid inference.
   b. No, this is not a valid inference.

_____ 9. Fed and Ginger practiced long hours on their dance routines.
   a. Yes, this is a valid inference.
   b. No, this is not a valid inference.

___ 10. Many romantic comedies and musical films followed an established blueprint for their plots.
   a. Yes, this is a valid inference.
   b. No, this is not a valid inference.

PRACTICE TESTS FOR

FLORIDA COLLEGE BASIC SKILLS EXIT READING TEST

TEXAS HIGHER EDUCATION ASSESSMENT TEST

THE SKILLED READER

AWARENESS INVENTORIES

FLORIDA COLLEGE BASIC SKILLS EXIT TEST

TEXAS HIGHER EDUCATION ASSESSMENT TEST

DIAGNOSTIC TEST FOR *THE SKILLED READER*

SUMMARY SHEET OF SCORES

Name _____ Date _____

Objective: To practice for the *Florida College Basic Skills Exit Reading Test*.

Take the practice test, *Florida College Basic Skills Exit Reading Test*, in your textbook. Fill
in the correct answer for each numbered item. Be sure to choose only one answer for each numbered item.

_____ 1. _____ 15. _____ 28.

_____ 2. _____ 16. _____ 29.

_____ 3. _____ 17. _____ 30.

_____ 4. _____ 18. _____ 31.

_____ 5. _____ 19. _____ 32.

_____ 6. _____ 20. _____ 33.

_____ 7. _____ 21. _____ 34.

_____ 8. _____ 22. _____ 35.

_____ 9. _____ 23. _____ 36.

_____ 10. _____ 24. _____ 37.

_____ 11. _____ 25. _____ 38.

_____ 12. _____ 26. _____ 39.

_____ 13. _____ 27. _____ 40.

_____ 14.

Name _____ Date _____

Objective: To gain more practice for the *Florida College Basic Skills Exit Reading Test.*

Fill in the correct answer for each numbered item. Be sure to choose only one answer for each numbered item.

_____ 1. _____ 15. _____ 28.

_____ 2. _____ 16. _____ 29.

_____ 3. _____ 17. _____ 30.

_____ 4. _____ 18. _____ 31.

_____ 5. _____ 19. _____ 32.

_____ 6. _____ 20. _____ 33.

_____ 7. _____ 21. _____ 34.

_____ 8. _____ 22. _____ 35.

_____ 9. _____ 23. _____ 36.

_____ 10. _____ 24. _____ 37.

_____ 11. _____ 25. _____ 38.

_____ 12. _____ 26. _____ 39.

_____ 13. _____ 27. _____ 40.

_____ 14.

Name _____ Date _____

Objective: To practice for the *Texas Higher Education Assessment Test*.

Take the practice test, *Texas Higher Education Assessment Test*, in your textbook. Fill in the correct answer for each numbered item. Be sure to choose only one answer for each numbered item.

_____ 1.	_____ 15.	_____ 28.
_____ 2.	_____ 16.	_____ 29.
_____ 3.	_____ 17.	_____ 30.
_____ 4.	_____ 18.	_____ 31.
_____ 5.	_____ 19.	_____ 32.
_____ 6.	_____ 20.	_____ 33.
_____ 7.	_____ 21.	_____ 34.
_____ 8.	_____ 22.	_____ 35.
_____ 9.	_____ 23.	_____ 36.
_____ 10.	_____ 24.	_____ 37.
_____ 11.	_____ 25.	_____ 38.
_____ 12.	_____ 26.	_____ 39.
_____ 13.	_____ 27.	_____ 40.
_____ 14.		

PRACTICE TEST FOR THE TEXAS HIGHER EDUCATION ASSESSMENT TEST

Name _____ Date _____

Objective: To gain more practice for the *Texas Higher Education Assessment Test*.

Fill in the correct answer for each numbered item. Be sure to choose only one answer for each numbered item.

_____ 1._____ 15. _____ 28.

_____ 2._____ 16. _____ 29.

_____ 3._____ 17. _____ 30.

_____ 4._____ 18. _____ 31.

_____ 5._____ 19. _____ 32.

_____ 6._____ 20. _____ 33.

_____ 7._____ 21. _____ 34.

_____ 8._____ 22. _____ 35.

_____ 9._____ 23. _____ 36.

_____ 10._____ 24. _____ 37.

_____ 11._____ 25. _____ 38.

_____ 12._____ 26. _____ 39.

_____ 13._____ 27. _____ 40.

_____ 14.

168

Name _____ Date _____

Objective: To discover strengths and areas for improvement in reading comprehension and critical reading.

Take the practice test for *The Skilled Reader*, in your textbook. Fill in the correct answer for each numbered item. Be sure to choose only one answer for each numbered item.

_____ 1. _____ 15. _____ 28.

_____ 2. _____ 16. _____ 29.

_____ 3. _____ 17. _____ 30.

_____ 4. _____ 18. _____ 31.

_____ 5. _____ 19. _____ 32.

_____ 6. _____ 20. _____ 33.

_____ 7. _____ 21. _____ 34.

_____ 8. _____ 22. _____ 35.

_____ 9. _____ 23. _____ 36.

_____ 10. _____ 24. _____ 37.

_____ 11. _____ 25. _____ 38.

_____ 12. _____ 26. _____ 39.

_____ 13. _____ 27. _____ 40.

_____ 14.

Name _____ Date _____

Objective: To discover strengths and areas for improvement in reading comprehension and critical reading.

Fill in the correct answer for each numbered item. Be sure to choose only one answer for each numbered item.

_____ 1.	_____ 15.	_____ 28.
_____ 2.	_____ 16.	_____ 29.
_____ 3.	_____ 17.	_____ 30.
_____ 4.	_____ 18.	_____ 31.
_____ 5.	_____ 19.	_____ 32.
_____ 6.	_____ 20.	_____ 33.
_____ 7.	_____ 21.	_____ 34.
_____ 8.	_____ 22.	_____ 35.
_____ 9.	_____ 23.	_____ 36.
_____ 10.	_____ 24.	_____ 37.
_____ 11.	_____ 25.	_____ 38.
_____ 12.	_____ 26.	_____ 39.
_____ 13.	_____ 27.	_____ 40.
_____ 14.		

Name _____ Date _____

Scores: % Correct   % Correct

Passage A   _____   Passage E   _____

Passage B   _____   Passage F   _____

Passage C   _____   Passage G   _____

Passage D   _____

The Reading Section of the *Florida State Basic Skills Exit Test* is based on the skills listed below. Circle the number of questions that you missed. Locate pages in your textbook that will help you develop each specific skill. Write out a study plan.

Passage/Question #	Skill
A4, A5, D6, E4, F4, G3	**Determine the meaning of words and phrases**.
AI, A7, CI, D2, EI, E4, GI, G6, FI, F2	**Understand the main idea and supporting details in written material**.
A2, A3, B2, B3, C2, D3, D5, E2, F3, G2, G5	**Identify a writer's purpose, point of view, and intended meaning**.
A6, DI, E3, F5	**Analyze the relationship among ideas in written material**.
B4, C3, D4, G4	**Use critical reasoning skills to evaluate written material**.
BI, F7	**Apply study skills to reading assignments**.

171

Plan of Action:

_____

_____

_____

_____

_____

_____

_____

_____

_____

_____

_____

_____

_____

_____

_____

_____

_____

_____

_____

_____

Name _____ Date _____

Scores: % Correct   % Correct

Passage A   _____   Passage E   _____

Passage B   _____   Passage F   _____

Passage C   _____   Passage G   _____

Passage D   _____

The Reading Section of the THEA Test is based on the skills listed below. Circle the number of questions that you missed. Locate pages in your textbook that will help you develop each specific skill. Write out a study plan.

Passage/Question #	Skill
A4, A5, D6, E4, F4, G3	**Determine the meaning of words and phrases.**
AI, A7, CI, D2, EI, E4, GI, G6, FI, F2	**Understand the main idea and supporting details in written material.**
A2, A3, B2, B3, C2, D3, D5, E2, F3, G2, G5	**Identify a writer's purpose, point of view, and intended meaning.**
A6, DI, E3, F5	**Analyze the relationship among ideas in written material.**
B4, C3, D4, G4	**Use critical reasoning skills to evaluate written material.**
BI, F7	**Apply study skills to reading assignments.**

Plan of Action:

_____

_____

_____

_____

_____

_____

_____

_____

_____

_____

_____

_____

_____

_____

_____

_____

_____

Name _____ Date _____

Scores: % Correct   % Correct

Passage A   _____   Passage C   _____

Passage B   _____   Passage D   _____

The Diagnostic Test for *The Skilled Reader* is based on the skills listed below. Circle the number of questions that you missed. Locate pages in your textbook that will help you develop each specific skill. Write out a study plan.

Passage/Question #	Skill	Textbook Pages
A6, A7, B7, B8, C1, D5, D6	**Vocabulary**	_____
A1, A8, B2, C2, C4, D1	**Main idea**	_____
C3, C10, D9	**Supporting Details**	_____
A3, A4, B3, C6	**Thought Patterns**	_____
A5, B5, B6, C5, D7	**Transitions**	_____
A2, A9, C8, C9	**Tone and Purpose**	_____
A9, C7, D8	**Fact/Opinion**	_____
A10, B10, D2, D3, D4	**Inferences**	_____

Plan of Action:

_____

_____

_____

_____

_____

_____

_____

_____

_____

_____

_____

_____

_____

_____

_____

_____

_____

_____

_____

SUMMARY SHEET OF SCORES

	SCORE
Chapter 1: A Reading System for Skilled Readers	
Lab 1.1 Practice Exercise 1	
Lab 1.2 Practice Exercise 2	
Lab 1.3 Review Test 1	
Lab 1.4 Review Test 2	
Lab 1.5 Mastery Test 1	
Lab 1.6 Mastery Test 2	
Chapter 2: Vocabulary in Context	
Lab 2.1 Practice Exercise 1	
Lab 2.2 Practice Exercise 2	
Lab 2.3 Review Test 1	
Lab 2.4 Review Test 2	
Lab 2.5 Mastery Test 1	
Lab 2.6 Mastery Test 2	
Chapter 3: Vocabulary-Building Skills	
Lab 3.1 Practice Exercise 1	
Lab 3.2 Practice Exercise 2	
Lab 3.3 Review Test 1	
Lab 3.4 Review Test 2	
Lab 3.5 Mastery Test 1	
Lab 3.6 Mastery Test 2	
Chapter 4: Topics and Main Ideas	
Lab 4.1 Practice Exercise 1	
Lab 4.2 Practice Exercise 2	
Lab 4.3 Review Test 1	
Lab 4.4 Review Test 2	
Lab 4.5 Mastery Test 1	
Lab 4.6 Mastery Test 2	
Chapter 5: Locating Stated Main Ideas	
Lab 5.1 Practice Exercise 1	
Lab 5.2 Practice Exercise 2	
Lab 5.3 Review Test 1	
Lab 5.4 Review Test 2	
Lab 5.5 Mastery Test 1	
Lab 5.6 Mastery Test 2	
Chapter 6: Implied Main Ideas	
Lab 6.1 Practice Exercise 1	
Lab 6.2 Practice Exercise 2	
Lab 6.3 Review Test 1	
Lab 6.4 Review Test 2	
Lab 6.5 Mastery Test 1	
Lab 6.6 Mastery Test 2	
Chapter 7: Supporting Details, Outlines, and Concept Maps	
Lab 7.1 Practice Exercise 1	
Lab 7.2 Practice Exercise 2	